PRAISE FOR *NO MATTER WHAT*

"I have had the distinct privilege to personally benefit from 'Pastor Marty's' preaching for many decades. What a gift to the body of Christ *No Matter What* represents. It puts into print what has been powerfully preached from the pulpit. God has uniquely gifted the author to unpack the story behind the story for his hearers. *No Matter What* brings out the original intent of the Master storyteller in a compelling, convicting and challenging manner. Joseph's story, presented so eloquently in this book, contains the potential to change your story!"

—Jim Blake, Executive Director
Alliance Redwoods, Occidental, CA

"Joseph is my favorite Bible character. There is so much to admire and take note of. Over and over, Pastor Marty reminds us of two themes: 1) Joseph never lost his focus on God, and 2) the imitation of Joseph is not possible. Only through Christ can we know the person who shaped Joseph's life. May it be so for us as well?"

—Richard E. Bush, Director of Coach Training
Christian and Missionary Alliance

"Marty Berglund speaks with a true pastor's heart and makes the story of Joseph accessible to everyday people who are looking for practical, godly advice for some of life's many challenges."

—Dr. Steve Elliott
Author and Pastor of First Alliance Church

"Each page brings a simple reminder that no matter what we face in this life, it's only temporary. Greater things are yet to come. Keep putting one foot in front of the other and all your trust in God—no matter what!"

—Chaplain Captain Cliff Jones
Federal Bureau of Prisons &
United States Army Reserve

"This is no ordinary book about Joseph. It is solidly biblical and practical. You'll find God-sized encouragement and practical insights to help you live for God no matter what life throws at you. Uniquely, *No Matter What* tells the story about Joseph, your life and God—the one who can redeem every and any situation in your life—no matter what."

—Rev. Dave Krilov, Pastor of miniChurch and Small Groups
Fellowship Alliance Chapel

"Marty Berglund is a superb communicator. When he speaks, I always want to listen; and when he writes, you can be sure that he will make his points in a clear and compelling way. The Joseph narrative is one of the great stories of the Bible, and this book captures the major lessons of Joseph's life."   —John F. Soper, Senior Pastor
Ridgeway Alliance Church

"The life of Joseph is a remarkable narrative and a well-known one to Bible readers of any length of time. Pastor Marty's insights and teaching are fresh and inspiring. This book reminds me how relevant a life lived over three thousand years ago is today. Anyone who reads this— from a seasoned pastor to a new Christian to someone just checking out matters of faith— will know God is real and He is for them."

—Scott Warren, Pastor, First Baptist Church, Mount Holly, NJ

"Pastor Marty declares his admiration for Joseph in the very first sentence of this insightful study of a life well-lived, despite hardship and circumstance. Each chapter of the book explains why. Surely there is no better model of perseverance and faith in all of Scripture. Twenty-first century believers will do well to read this book prayerfully and allow the insights found on its pages to inspire them to follow Christ faithfully, as the author strives to do himself."

—Dan Wetzel, Vice President of Church Ministries
Christian Ministry Alliance

NO MATTER WHAT

Abiding in God's Faithfulness

Love Never fails

MARTY BERGLUND

CLC
PUBLICATIONS
Fort Washington, PA 19034

No Matter What
Published by CLC Publications

U.S.A.
P.O. Box 1449, Fort Washington, PA 19034

UNITED KINGDOM
CLC International (UK)
51 The Dean, Alresford, Hampshire, SO24 9BJ

© 2015 by Martin R. Berglund
All rights reserved. Published 2015.

ISBN (trade paper): 978-1-61958-199-9
ISBN (e-book): 978-1-61958-200-2

DEDICATION

This book is dedicated to my mom,
Eleanor Berglund Borg
and to Joseph's mom, Rachel.
You both did good!
Thanks.

CONTENTS

ACKNOWLEDGEMENTS

I actually feel a sense of excitement about acknowledging others who helped me put this book together because they deserve so much credit for getting it to print. For me, this is an opportunity to give honor to them, and deep thanks for all they did to get this into your hands.

The first person I must thank encouraged me, helped me and guided me the most in this process: Donna Thomas. She is an amazing editor and has great God-given insight into the minds and hearts of others as they long to connect to God. Donna has many years of experience in the newspaper industry and had all the tools needed to help in completing this work.

As you read this book that was birthed through sermons spoken at Fellowship Alliance Chapel, you will notice that two other pastors on our staff contributed by adding chapters. Pastor Don Hay is gifted to see deeply into the developmental processes people go through. He gives us insights into the many changes Joseph went through. Pastor Mike Williams, a youth pastor for many years, helps us understand the relational dynamics that framed and formed Joseph from childhood into adulthood.

Many others along the way helped put this book together so you could be inspired and hopefully changed in deep spiritual ways by reading and applying all you learn.

Probably the one I truly need to acknowledge most is Joseph, the son of Jacob. Someday, when I meet him in heaven (he is on my top ten list of people I want to meet there), I will tell him that his life commitment to the Lord profoundly changed my life. I can't wait to thank him myself.

Chapter 1

GOD'S PLAN AND YOUR LIFE

Genesis 37

Marty Berglund

Trust God's plan for your life!

I want to be like Joseph. I hope that when you finish this book, you will want to be like Joseph, too.

Here's the story of a man who faced every hardship you can imagine—betrayal, imprisonment, pain, temptation, a dysfunctional family (perhaps the most dysfunctional of all time!)—yet he never lost his focus on God. Joseph knew that God had a plan for his life, and he rested firmly on the promise that God would never leave him—never!

I want to be like that. I need to be like that. Imagine the difference in your life if you could be like that.

As we journey through this story, there are many lessons for us, lessons we can apply right now, that will help us be more like Joseph—*no matter what.* That's a phrase I can hang on to—"no matter what." If your life is anything like mine, the "no matter whats" are coming faster than you can handle. No time to waste here, so let's get started!

Genesis 36 recounts the lineage of Esau, which is not a pretty story. Isaac had two sons, Esau and Jacob. Jacob ended up following God's plan, but Esau—well, not so much. Though he did some things well, mostly Esau was focused on his own plan and his own wants. His story shows the impact one man can have when he chooses not to follow God's plan.

In chapter 37, we see just the opposite: the impact one man can have when he does follow God's plan. From this chapter to the end of Genesis, we learn about Joseph—and there is a lot to learn. Multiple generations are changed, all because of one man. It reminds me of the vision statement of my church: we want people to hear God's call and follow it.

Responding to God's call is a concept based on the distinctly biblical premise that God has a plan for our lives. Other religions of the world do not conceive of God as interested in individuals. Their god (or gods) may have a plan, but it's a general plan; the role of the individual is simply to do whatever can be done to appease their god. But the idea that God has a personal plan for your life is all over the Bible and dramatically visible in the life of Joseph.

God does have a plan for your life—a plan to bless you, to guide you, to make your life fulfilling. Without God and His plan, life has no meaning or purpose. That's what makes hell so hellish—it is meaningless and purposeless.

My hope and dream for you—and everyone reading this book—is that you will trust God's plan for your life. God wants to bless you, to use you, to fulfill you—but only if you are willing to join His plan.

So let's examine Chapter 37 and see what happens in Joseph's life as he chooses to follow God's plan, for therein lies his, and our, hope.

God Has a Plan to Bless You

The unfolding of God's plan is evident right at the beginning of the chapter:

> Jacob lived in the land of his father's sojournings, in the land of Canaan. These are the generations of Jacob. Joseph, being seventeen years old, was pasturing the flock with his brothers. He was a boy with the sons of Bilhah and Zilpah, his father's wives. And Joseph brought a bad report of them to their father. (Gen. 37:1–2)

Joseph, a boy of seventeen, brings a bad report about his brothers to their father. Is he being a tattletale? Is he trying to get some respect, being the little brother? Or is he concerned about telling the truth? Let's read on, and you can judge for yourself.

> Now Israel loved Joseph more than any other of his sons, because he was the son of his old age. And he made him a robe of many colors. But when his brothers saw that their father loved him more than all his brothers, they hated him and could not speak peacefully to him. (37:3–4)

That says a lot. Jacob is in denial about how his sons are relating to each other—so much so that he shows favoritism to his younger son. Both the Bible and psychology agree that showing favoritism to one child over another creates jealousy and hatred, just as we see in this story.

Jacob only makes things worse by giving his favorite son a "coat of many colors"—an ornamental garment of the kind worn by royalty and people who don't work for a living. How do you think his brothers, who are slaving away as shepherds, feel about that? It is hard to believe that Jacob could be so stupid, so out of touch with reality, that he would show such favoritism and give his boys multiple reasons to hate Joseph. Jacob is in denial about issues in his own family.

But Jacob is not alone. Joseph is also in denial:

> Now Joseph had a dream, and when he told it to his broth-ers they hated him even more. He said to them, "Hear this dream that I have dreamed: Behold, we were binding sheaves in the field, and behold, my sheaf arose and stood upright. And behold, your sheaves gathered around it and bowed down to my sheaf." His brothers said to him, "Are you indeed to reign over us? Or are you indeed to rule over us?" So they hated him even more for his dreams and for his words. Then he dreamed another dream and told it to his brothers and said, "Behold, I have dreamed another dream. Behold, the sun, the moon, and eleven stars were bowing down to me." But when he told it to his father and to his brothers, his father rebuked him and said to him, "What is this dream that you have dreamed? Shall I and your mother and your brothers indeed come to bow our-selves to the ground before you?" And his brothers were jealous of him, but his father kept the saying in mind. (Gen. 37:5–11)

Joseph's brothers already "hated him and could not speak peacefully to him." Why, then, doesn't he realize that tell-ing them his dreams will only make matters worse? Can you imagine the family atmosphere? People won't talk to each other, or when they do, it's biting and critical. If you've ever lived in a family like this, you know how bad it can be. And it's all because of Jacob's refusal to address issues and Jo-seph's denial and naiveté in dealing with his brothers.

God wants to bless you when you join His plan, but if you live in denial about issues in your life that God wants you to address, you ruin the blessing. Why isn't God taking care of you? Why are you unhappy? Could it be that you're supposed to be addressing issues in your life, but you are in denial? It's a scary thought, isn't it? But it's right there in the story: Jacob and Joseph wouldn't address their issues. They wanted to live in "la-la land," so they didn't have the blessing of God.

This family sounds totally dysfunctional, doesn't it? Yet these are the people of God! God's blessing is not coming through in their lives because they're in denial. Imagine what would have happened if Jacob had been honest with his sons, and if Joseph had been more honest with himself. If they had been more open about their own issues, I wonder if Joseph's dreams would have been different.

If you've read the book of Genesis, you know that Joseph's dreams eventually come true, that Jacob's family is saved from famine, and that eventually (as the story continues in the book of Exodus) God is going to rescue the people of Israel from slavery in Egypt. I wonder if all that would have had to happen if Jacob and Joseph had addressed their issues.

I wonder, in your family, if some of your painful experiences really had to happen, or if it was just because you're living in denial. If you really got honest before God, His plan for blessing could come on your life. I'm not trying to put you under guilt; I'm just trying to ask, *are you really being honest with God?*

I have a friend named Pete Scazzero who is a pastor in Queens, New York, in one of the wealthiest ethnic communities on earth. He grew up in an Italian home in North Jersey, became a Christian in college, trained for the ministry and started a church in Queens in 1987. He even learned Spanish so he could better serve his community. Pete is a Type-A personality, a make-it-happen kind of a guy. He's amazing.

But by 1996, Pete was burned out. He was working day and night at the church, trying everything he could to make it grow. It was growing, but there were problems that finally resulted in a split in the church. Pete had the same problem as Jacob—he was in denial. There were things in his life he should have addressed, such as the tension in his marriage, but he didn't.

Pete's wife, Geri, came to him one day and said, "Honey, I'm quitting the church. I can't take it anymore." Pete hit rock bottom. He went to the elders in his church, confessed the whole situation and they decided that Pete and Geri should get Christian professional help. They sent them off on a week-long intensive counseling session to see if they could find out what was at the bottom of this and work it out.

With all his church responsibilities, Pete was hoping for a quick end to the situation. That wasn't to be. During these sessions, they didn't feel safe enough to speak their minds. Finally one night, Geri woke Pete up using, as he said, "a few choice words." She let Pete have it. For the first time, Geri told her husband the brutal truth about everything—him, the church and their marriage. She let it all out.

What followed was a spiritual awakening for both of them. They never expected to experience the blessings of

God in such a situation. But as they talked and listened to each other—deeply listened, perhaps for the first time—they found that they had been living in denial about so many things.

They had been Christians for twenty years and had founded a successful church, but even though their marriage looked good from the outside, they had only let Jesus in just so far, and that "so far" was not nearly deep enough. They discovered truths about themselves as well as their church. They stopped denying and started opening up to what God had in store, and the blessings started to flow. From the lessons God taught him during this time, he wrote a book, *The Emotionally Healthy Church.*[1]

That's what this story is about. You should be experiencing the blessing, but you're not. Where's the joy? Where's the fulfillment? Is God trying to get you to deal with something, but you keep living in denial?

It is so hard sometimes for the Lord to get hold of us, isn't it? Pete and Geri were sold out for the Lord, but God had to deal with some issues in their life. It had to happen to them; maybe it needs to happen to you.

We sometimes call this brokenness. It's all about surrendering to God's plan and putting your plans on the shelf. I hope it happens to you, no matter what crisis it takes, because it's the only chance for your life to have meaning and purpose. That leads us to our second point.

God Has a Plan to Protect You

Why are we afraid to address issues? Because we're not sure we are going to be protected. Look what happens as Joseph's story continues:

> Now his brothers went to pasture their father's flock near Shechem. And Israel said to Joseph, "Are not your brothers pasturing the flock at Shechem? Come, I will send you to them." And he said to him, "Here I am." So he said to him, "Go now, see if it is well with your brothers and with the flock, and bring me word." So he sent him from the Valley of Hebron, and he came to Shechem. And a man found him wandering in the fields. And the man asked him, "What are you seeking?" "I am seeking my brothers," he said. "Tell me, please, where they are pasturing the flock." And the man said, "They have gone away, for I heard them say, 'Let us go to Dothan.'" So Joseph went after his brothers and found them at Dothan. They saw him from afar, and before he came near to them they conspired against him to kill him. They said to one another, "Here comes this dreamer. Come now, let us kill him and throw him into one of the pits. Then we will say that a fierce animal has devoured him, and we will see what will become of his dreams." (Gen. 37:12–20)

Isn't it amazing what a little jealousy, envy, anger and pride can get someone to do—things they never thought they would do? It's scary how evil the human heart can get, to actually think about killing your brother! It's a sad story, but it's so real, isn't it? Maybe you've done things like that in your life, and you said later, "I don't know what I was thinking!" I know what you were thinking: jealousy, pride, envy, anger. It's been with humanity forever. And unless you address those sins, they can take you to places you don't want to go.

> But when Reuben heard it, he rescued him out of their hands, saying, "Let us not take his life." And Reuben said to them, "Shed no blood, throw him into this pit here in

the wilderness, but do not lay a hand on him"—that he might rescue him out of their hand to restore him to his father. So when Joseph came to his brothers, they stripped him of his robe, the robe of many colors that he wore. And they took him and threw him into a pit. The pit was empty; there was no water in it. Then they sat down to eat. And looking up they saw a caravan of Ishmaelites coming from Gilead with their camels bearing gum, balm, and myrrh on their way to carry it down to Egypt. Then Judah said to his brothers, "What profit is it if we kill our brother and conceal his blood? Come, let us sell him to the Ishmaelites, and let not our hand be upon him, for he is our brother, our own flesh." And his brothers listened to him. Then Midianite traders passed by. And they drew Joseph up and lifted him out of the pit, and sold him to the Ishmaelites for twenty shekels of silver. They took Joseph to Egypt. (Gen 37:21–28)

When I read this story, it brings questions to my mind about how God wants to protect His children. God has promised throughout Scripture that He is going to protect Israel. Yet one of the brothers gets sold into slavery in Egypt. What does this say about the protection of God? How about Christians who have been injured or even killed in accidents, or diagnosed with cancer or suffer through other problems and difficulties? Where's the protection of God?

Have you ever asked those questions? If you read the Bible honestly, you find that, yes, sometimes God protects, rescues and heals. But you also see John the Baptist getting his head cut off. You see Stephen getting stoned to death. It seems that sometimes God physically protects, and sometimes He doesn't. So what does the protection of God really mean? Can you count on it or not?

The answer is that God wants to protect you in the greatest way possible. He wants to protect you from a meaningless, purposeless, nothing life! Remember, that's what makes hell so hellish. The greatest protection God can offer you is to have His plan, His purpose, His meaning for your life—whether that means you live or you die.

This is what the apostle Paul says in Romans 14:8: "For if we live, we live to the Lord, and if we die, we die to the Lord. So then, whether we live or whether we die, we are the Lord's." Do you see what he's saying? If I'm in God's plan, I have something to live for. If not, I really have nothing. Even if I win all the games, have all the possessions and go wherever I want, I've got nothing.

The protection of God is the greatest protection you can have. It's a protection of the meaning, purpose, significance and fulfillment in your life.

One of the most amazing things we see in a Bible story like this is how God works out His plan. He doesn't just impose His purpose on humanity; He works through humans—their ups and downs, their failures and successes. It is unbelievable how God does this. He doesn't just have an overall plan; He has a plan for individuals as well, and it all coincides. It's a stroke of genius, and only God can do it.

When I was struck down with the Epstein-Barr virus in 1992, I questioned God's plan. I could hardly think straight. I could hardly be a husband to my wife or a father to my kids. I was 40 years old and my life seemed to be over. I was thinking, "I don't really like Your plan, Lord!" Then somebody gave me a book by Elisabeth Elliot called *A Path Through Suffering*.

Elisabeth Elliot was a missionary who gave her life to serve the Lord in South America among the Waorani (then called "Auca") Indians. A group of Waorani killed her husband and four others. *Was this really the plan of God?* she wondered. She wondered the same thing when her second husband died. If anyone has a right to ask this question, it's Elisabeth Elliot.

The major thing she taught me in that book is that suffering is really, really hard—if it's meaningless. But if there is a reason, if there is a God and He has a purpose in your suffering, it changes everything. Elisabeth looked at all her sufferings and came to the conclusion that it only made sense if everything she encountered in life, both good and bad, had meaning in God's plan. Then, she concluded, "they were worth it."[2]

That was a powerful message for me back then and, I hope, a powerful message for you. Have you grabbed hold of that yet? Or are you still trying to work your way around difficulties and stay away from pain? That's not what the Christian life is supposed to be. What it's all about is finding God's plan for your life. There's protection *only* in God's plan.

God Has a Plan to Temper You

When Reuben returned to the pit and saw that Joseph was not in the pit, he tore his clothes and returned to his brothers and said, "The boy is gone, and I, where shall I go?" Then they took Joseph's robe and slaughtered a goat and dipped the robe in the blood. And they sent the robe of many colors and brought it to their father and said, "this we have found; please identify whether it is your son's robe or not." And he identified it and said, "It is my son's robe. A fierce animal has devoured him. Joseph is

without doubt torn to pieces." Then Jacob tore his gar-
ments and put sackcloth on his loins and mourned for his
son many days. All his sons and all his daughters rose up
to comfort him, but he refused to be comforted and said,
"No, I shall go down to Sheol to my son, mourning." Thus
his father wept for him. Meanwhile the Midianites had
sold him in Egypt to Potiphar, an officer of Pharaoh, the
captain of the guard. (Gen. 37:29–36)

God has a plan to *temper* you. That's what God is doing to
Jacob here, as well as to Joseph. The word *temper* means "to
soften by the addition or influence of a moderating element."
It's changing your idealism to realism—that's what's going
on here.

Notice they slaughtered a goat. If you remember, Jacob
used a goat skin to deceive his father and get the blessing.
Now his own sons use a goat's blood to deceive Jacob. The
apple doesn't fall far from the tree, does it? Jacob deceived
his dad, now his sons deceive him. Nobody confronts their
issues—they are all in denial.

One person is honest, though, and that's Joseph. He's the
only hope for this family. If just one person can turn to God
and surrender to His plan, he can change entire generations
to come. That's what we learn from this story.

Verse 35 says that no one could comfort Jacob. Isn't this
the ultimate cruelty? The brothers convince Dad that Joe is
dead, when they know he is still alive. Dad is crying his eyes
out, in sackcloth and ashes, and they just let it happen. You
would think that they would break down and admit what really happened, but they don't. It's just plain evil.

And yet, God uses this evil in a powerful way in Jacob's
life. Jacob hasn't always been an admirable person, but by

the end of the book of Genesis he finishes strong. And Joseph, by the end of this book, even says to his brothers, "You meant it for evil, but God meant it for good." Really? This wicked thing? Yes. God can even use the wickedness of man in His plan, when people surrender like Joseph did.

Something may have taken place in your life that just seems insane, painful, even stupid. And you ask, "How can God use this?" Don't worry, God can do anything.

My father-in-law, Paul Bubna, was quite a guy. He could apply Romans 8:28 to almost any situation. He embraced it. In all things, Paul truly believed that "God is working together for our personal good." That can be hard to accept at times, extremely difficult at others. But Paul knew the secret. He was always aware of his responses to situations and God's larger calling upon his life. He didn't believe things "just happened"; everything had a purpose in God's plan.

One of our favorite family stories about Paul is when he took his first pastorate. Married about a year, just out of college, they were called to a small parish in Kansas. July in Kansas can be very hot and the humidity was through the roof. They moved into a run-down parsonage that needed a lot of work.

So they went to town to buy some bare-bones furniture. Paul borrowed a trailer from a neighboring farmer and they loaded it up with secondhand furniture. On the way back to their new home, the mattress that was stacked on top of everything shifted and rolled off into a ditch. When they noticed it was gone, they tried to turn around to go back and pick it up.

Paul was a city boy and had never driven with a trailer before, so it's not hard to imagine what happened. He jack-knifed that thing in the middle of the highway. Part of the trailer came up over the rear bumper and the bolt that was holding the trailer got stuck. The corner of the trailer was up against the trunk of the car, denting it—a car they had just paid to have painted. The only way to fix the situation was to jack up the car, but they couldn't get to the trunk.

It was about 105 degrees. They knew that their mattress was lying in a ditch, maybe even in water, back along the highway. Now they had to figure out how to get a jackknifed trailer unstuck so they could go retrieve it. Being the godly man that he was, Paul reached for God's Word, opened it and read, "He came that we might have life and have it more abundantly." Laughing, Paul said it did not seem to immediately apply at that moment!

We can all identify with circumstances in our lives where God's promises of abundant living seem far from us—just as they seemed far from Joseph and Jacob at this point in the story. And that's why this story was written—to prove to you and me that God has a plan and He's working it out. Your only hope of security, significance, meaning and purpose in life is to join His plan.

That means, of course, that you have to surrender *your* plan. And that's where this chapter ends. The only way to have God's plan for your life is to cash in yours. You can't have both.

I'll never forget my old theology professor back in Bible college, leaning on the lectern, peering at us over his glasses, and saying, "Students, don't you ever deny in the dark what

God showed you in the light." And that's where Jacob is right now. God made promises to him, but he's in a dark place right now. He can deny it or he can believe God's got a plan.

You're in the same place. Even on a highway with your stupid car jackknifed across it, can you believe God's got a plan? Can you laugh a little and say, "All right, I don't get it, but God, I surrender"? In the tragedy of a lost child or difficulties in your marriage, can you believe God's plan and trust Him for it?

Prayer

Lord, am I in denial? Are there issues in my life that you have wanted me to address for years and I've never really confronted them? Lord, let it begin with me. I can be that person that changes my entire family. Lord, I'm ready, I'm willing, I'm here. Teach me. Take me step by step. Whatever you want, I'll do it. It's all about You and following in Your plan. I see now, Lord, it's only with You and Your plan that I can have any meaning and purpose to my life. Otherwise it's all nonsense. Lord, all my hopes and dreams for my life, my health, my kids—God, I put them on Your altar and I accept Your plan. I'm going to believe Your purpose and Your meaning in everything that happens. Your protection is protecting me from a meaningless life. I hold on to that with all my strength and I hold on to You. In the name of Jesus Christ, I pray. Amen.

Chapter 2

A LIFE OF GREAT RESULTS

Genesis 39

Marty Berglund

Focusing your life on the Lord produces great results!
We will see this profoundly displayed in the life of Joseph.

My job as a preacher is to equip the church. Ephesians 4 says that apostles, prophets, evangelists, shepherds and teachers are:

> to equip the saints for the work of ministry, for building
> up the body of Christ . . . to mature manhood . . . Rather,
> speaking the truth in love, we are to grow up in every
> way into him who is the head, into Christ, from whom the
> whole body, joined and held together by every joint with
> which it is equipped, when each part is working properly,
> makes the body grow so that it builds itself up in love.
> (4:12–16)

There are some really glorious results in that passage but the results hinge on whether the teachers and preachers are doing their jobs. If you are ready to be equipped, let's continue in the story of Joseph. I can guarantee that by looking at Joseph we will find some equipment for life and ministry, and the results you desperately want and need in your life.

Great Success

Let's look at the first six verses of Genesis 39:

> Now Joseph had been brought down to Egypt, and Potiphar, an officer of Pharaoh, the captain of the guard, an Egyptian, had bought him from the Ishmaelites who had brought him down there. The Lord was with Joseph, and he became a successful man, and he was in the house of his Egyptian master. His master saw that the Lord was with him and that the Lord caused all that he did to succeed in his hands. So Joseph found favor in his sight and attended him, and he made him overseer of his house and put him in charge of all that he had. From the time that he made him overseer in his house and over all that he had the Lord blessed the Egyptian's house for Joseph's sake; the blessing of the Lord was on all that he had, in house and field. So he left all that he had in Joseph's charge, and because of him he had no concern about anything but the food he ate. (39:1–6)

Joseph had been sold into slavery by his big brothers, and Potiphar, a captain of the Egyptian guard, had bought him. Throughout his journey so far, Joseph had no place to go but to the Lord. By the time he got to Egypt, Joseph and the Lord were very close.

Look at verse 2: "and the Lord was with Joseph, and he became a successful man." Success and slavery don't usually go together. But Joseph was a really successful slave. That's what Joseph was like: anywhere you put him, he made a difference. Any circumstance you put him in, he changed it. Any trial you put him in, he came out on top. He's a success, even though he's a slave. Do you think you would be?

In our world today, the normal reaction for someone in Joseph's situation would be to dwell on the surroundings and circumstances—a new country with strange food, strange people and strange customs. Betrayed by your brothers and sold into slavery, you are living a life that is a far cry from what you had imagined. Depressed and despairing, you might turn to drugs or alcohol to cope. The next thing you know, you're in jail or dead. Isn't that the norm?

And yet Joseph totally defies the norm. How does he do it? I suggest it was because of his focus.

As the title of this chapter suggests, focusing your life on the Lord produces results—results of success. Joseph is a great illustration of that. No matter the situation or circumstances he finds himself in, Joseph remains focused on the Lord.

What else could he focus on? Well, he could have focused on how he was betrayed by his brothers—that's depressing. Or how much he missed his dad and his home, which would certainly bring him down. Or he could have focused on the fact that he was a slave, with no wife, no kids, no home of his own—there's a painful thought. He could have focused on how his life seemed wasted now, with absolutely nothing working out for him. Who could blame Joseph if he had focused on his extremely bad luck? His future was looking pretty grim.

But Joseph doesn't let his pain, his circumstances or his difficulties define him. That is a rare and unusual attitude. His circumstances have not changed dramatically since the day his brothers threw him in the well, but they are beginning to change at this point. Though still a slave, he has acquired some authority.

And it's all because he kept his focus on the Lord. Did you notice that the passage says "the Lord" five times in six verses? That's what made all the difference in the world: Joseph's focus was on the Lord. Even his pagan boss notices and says to himself, "The Lord blesses this kid no matter where I put him, so I'm going to put him in charge of all I've got." Even a pagan can see it! This is phenomenal.

Let's ask the question again: *why?* Why does the Lord bless him so much? I think it's because of his humility, his brokenness, his willingness to surrender to the Lord. This is how Jesus opens his Sermon on the Mount in Matthew 5, 6 and 7—what many call the greatest sermon ever preached: "Blessed are the poor in spirit."

Really? The weak, the humble, the powerless are *blessed?* Yes—those who are focused on the Lord, who realize their own bankruptcy and know that they can't do it on their own.

We tell people in trying circumstances, "You can handle it; suck it up and be strong," but that's a bunch of hogwash. That's not how Joseph made it. He made it by focusing on the Lord. Recognizing that he didn't have the power to change his circumstances, he humbled himself before the Lord. That's why this text says "the Lord, the Lord, the Lord" over and over again. The Lord can bless this young man because he's focused on Him.

In his book *What Jesus Said about Successful Living*, Haddon Robinson tells the story of his dad as he aged, became senile and moved in with Haddon. After a series of extremely frustrating events, Haddon displayed his anger at his dad in an altercation that involved a little "swatting." Later, in his remorse for his actions, Haddon had a revelation from God. He said it was horrible—he got a glimpse of the ugliness inside of himself that day. He realized the depravity and bankruptcy of his own life.

Haddon said that he wished his dad were alive today so he could apologize, but he admitted that he couldn't really say he didn't mean it because, at that moment, he did. He could have excused it and said, "Well, old people get that way and can be irritating." But he discovered the truth about himself—that inside him was just a flash of a murderer. Haddon concluded that we can either wipe such self-knowledge from our minds and travel on, or we can realize the poverty of our own spirits and throw ourselves at His feet and beg for mercy and forgiveness.

"We all need the grace of a forgiving God," Robinson writes. "Those who understand this make it into the kingdom of God. As Samuel Rutherford said, 'Bow low, man, bow low. The door to the kingdom is low.'"[1]

Joseph must have understood that. To be so blessed of God in everything he did, he had to realize his own bankruptcy, his own poverty of spirit. And this is where you and I need to go if we are ever going to be blessed of God. It is recognizing humbly that "I can't pull it off, I can't do it. But the Lord can! I'm going to focus on the Lord."

Joseph was a slave in a foreign land, where he was considered worthless in their minds. And yet, as he focused on the Lord, Joseph was elevated. That's something to think about.

Great Character

As the story continues, trouble is looming for Joseph:

> Now Joseph was handsome in form and appearance. And
> after a time his master's wife cast her eyes on Joseph and
> said, "Lie with me." But he refused and said to his master's
> wife, "Behold, because of me my master has no concern
> about anything in the house, and he has put everything
> that he has in my charge. He is not greater in this house
> than I am, nor has he kept back anything from me except
> yourself, because you are his wife. How then can I do this
> great wickedness and sin against God?" And as she spoke
> to Joseph day after day, he would not listen to her, to lie
> beside her or to be with her. (Gen. 39:6–10)

Joseph was handsome, both inside and out, and Mrs. Potiphar noticed that. We can imagine that he was lonely and
stressed out by all the pressure of running the household,
and he probably could have used someone to comfort him,
talk to him and just be with him. This woman (who may have
been old enough to be his mother, I don't know) comes after
him time and time again, but Joseph doesn't fall for it. He still
resists—amazing.

How do you think he did it? There is a clue in verse 9:
"How then can I do this great wickedness and sin against
God?" Joseph knew it would be a sin against his master,
against his master's wife, against himself. But who was his
focus on? "I don't want to sin against God."

I'm a pastor, and people come to me when they've been
caught in a sin—something illegal, unethical or immoral.
They may seem repentant when they talk about what they've
done. But when they talk more about what other people are
going to think or what they're going to look like to others, I

get worried, because their focus is still on themselves and on everyone else.

However, when I see them crying and weeping because of what they have done to betray Jesus—how they turned their backs on the Lord, how they've fallen away from the Lord—then I feel much better. I think to myself, "Okay, now you get it." I love it when I'm talking to somebody and they don't care what other people think, because what they are most concerned about is the Lord. Then I know this person is going to be okay.

When you sin, you don't just sin against people, circumstances or situations, or even yourself. You sin against God. You have fractured your relationship with God. That's what Joseph sees here! "I couldn't do this to the Lord after all He's done for me." His relationship with the Lord was so important he wouldn't fracture it, even for companionship he may have wanted or desired. This is the key. Let's read the rest of these verses and see what happens.

> But one day, when he went into the house to do his work and none of the men of the house was there in the house, she caught him by his garment, saying, "Lie with me." But he left his garment in her hand and fled and got out of the house. And as soon as she saw that he had left his garment in her hand and had fled out of the house, she called to the men of her household and said to them, "See, he has brought among us a Hebrew to laugh at us. He came in to me to lie with me, and I cried out with a loud voice. And as soon as he heard that I lifted up my voice and cried out, he left his garment beside me and fled and got out of the house." Then she laid up his garment by her until his master came home, and she told him the same story, saying, "The Hebrew servant, whom you have brought

> among us, came in to me to laugh at me. But as soon as I
> lifted up my voice and cried, he left his garment beside me
> and fled out of the house." (Gen. 39:11–18)

Here is a young man trying to keep his way pure, trying to flee youthful lust, and what happens? It doesn't go
well. Still, Joseph showed great character; he proved what he
was really made of. Temptation proves what you are really
about—whether you are truly serving the Lord or not.

What are we really talking about here? I called it character, but I'm talking about standing up to sexual sin. We
don't like to talk about how easy it can be to fall into an affair
or respond to flirtation, but I've been a pastor for over three
decades. You don't think I've been tempted many times with
a sensual glance or a flirtatious word? All I would have to
do is respond back. It is that easy. Many temptations are out
there, but I have resisted. I haven't had to physically flee, but
I would!

I have many pastoral friends who haven't fled and have
fallen into sin. I have wondered why I've done so well with
this and they haven't. I'm certainly not any better than they
are. Some of them were good friends, awesome guys—so how
did they fall? How did I not fall? Was it just my good marriage? Was it just that the circumstances weren't the same?

After talking with men like this and helping some of
them walk back out of that sin and get better, I noticed
something they all had in common: a loss of focus. Through
the stress of life, problems in their marriages or difficulties
in their walk with God, they lost their focus. And when you
lose your focus, you are bait for the devil. All he has to do is
throw a little temptation your way and you will fall.

Has that happened to you? I challenge you, I plead with you, go back to the Lord. Get away, cancel things, do whatever you've got to do to flee. Get tight with the Lord. That's the only way you can resist temptation and keep your ways pure. Have the kind of successful, God-honoring character that your kids can look back on and admire rather than be ashamed. That focus on the Lord is what gives you the strength to resist temptation. And Joseph had it.

Great Fulfillment

> As soon as his master heard the words that his wife spoke to him, "This is the way your servant treated me," his anger was kindled. And Joseph's master took him and put him into the prison, the place where the king's prisoners were confined, and he was there in prison. But the Lord was with Joseph and showed him steadfast love and gave him favor in the sight of the keeper of the prison. And the keeper of the prison put Joseph in charge of all the prisoners who were in the prison. Whatever was done there, he was the one who did it. The keeper of the prison paid no attention to anything that was in Joseph's charge, because the Lord was with him. And whatever he did, the Lord made it succeed. (Gen. 39:18–23)

Notice in verse 21 that important word "but." The master's wife tells a lie about Joseph, and he gets thrown in jail because his master is so angry. Now he's in prison—"*But* the Lord was with Joseph."

In this world, you may never be on top, never be the best at anything, never set records, never be recognized for your great gifts. *But* if you have the Lord, you have more than all men seek. Don't forget that! If you have the Lord, you have the joy, peace, power, patience, love, forgiveness and eternal life that no one in this world has, and which they all long for. You've got it in the Lord. Focus on that. Go deeper in your relationship with the Lord. Somehow, some way, Joseph just seemed to get that.

In Verse 23 it says it again: "because the Lord was with him." It reminds me of Hebrews 13:5: "Keep your life free from love of money, and be content with what you have, for he has said, 'I will never leave you nor forsake you.'"

The last part of that verse has unusual wording in the original Greek. If you translate it literally, it reads with *five* negatives (for emphasis): "I will not, not leave you; neither [not] will I not, not forsake you." Why is "not" repeated five times in that short little phrase? To emphasize to us that it is absolutely impossible. God won't leave you. Now, you might leave Him. But He won't leave you. He won't. He won't. He won't.

This is what Joseph depended upon. "The Lord's not going to leave me. Even if I am unjustly thrown in prison and all the cards seem stacked against me. Even if I have unbelievably bad luck, the Lord's not leaving me. The Lord's still here. He will not, not, not, not, not forsake me. He's here."

And He's there with you. If you get cancer, He's there with you. If you get divorced, He's there with you. If things are not working out, He's there with you. If you've got the Lord, you've really got everything! Joseph seemed to get that. Do you?

I don't know if you've noticed, but this whole chapter is about suffering unjustly—that's the life of Joseph in a nutshell. Talk about bad luck—your own brothers sell you into slavery, then just as things are going better, Potiphar's wife lies about you and you get thrown into prison. You can't seem to catch a break! Even though he's trying his best to be pure and focus on the Lord, Joseph finds himself suffering.

If you feel that you are suffering unjustly—"How come they get that and I don't?" "How come that happened to me?" "It's not fair!"—then this lesson is for you. None of what happened to Joseph was fair—none of it! But he kept his focus on the Lord. You do the same and things will be fine, you'll see.

What defines you? For many people it's their loss, their bad luck, their pain. That is not the Christian life, and it's not Joseph. He never let himself be defined as a slave, as a prisoner, as someone betrayed by his own brothers. Are you letting things like regret, sadness or depression define you?

Your focus is wrong—all wrong. You've got to focus on the Lord, like Joseph, who kept focusing on the Lord, *no matter what*. That's what I'm praying for you. May this be a defining moment for you, when you decide to stop defining your life by that person, that difficulty, that sickness, and look to the Lord.

Prayer

Lord, I can't do it, and I can't fix it, so Lord, I am going to focus on You. Help me to do that, Lord. I come before You now with deep humility, on my knees and in my heart. I look to You to take my life, with all its twists and turns, bad luck, difficulties, hardships and unfairness, and I give them all to You. I'm not going to define my life by that anymore. I'm going to define my life with "The Lord is with me and will not, not, not, not, not leave me—period." Amen.

Chapter 3

THE SECRET TO A GOOD LIFE

Genesis 40

Marty Berglund

The secret is serving.

The secret to a good life is found in our study of the life of Joseph—though at this point in the story, you may be wondering just how that can be.

Sold into slavery by his own brothers, Joseph arrives in Egypt and ends up in the household of Potiphar, who is so impressed with Joseph and his work ethic and attitude that he elevates him to be in charge of everything he owns! But Potiphar's wife becomes enamored with Joseph and tries to lure him into a compromising situation. He flees, leaving his cloak behind. Mrs. Potiphar, in anger at his rejection, accuses Joseph of attempted rape. Potiphar throws him into prison.

This is the good life?

What must it have been like in that prison? We've all heard stories about prisoners of war. Some of the worst stories I've ever read come from the Vietnam War, by American pilots captured and put into the infamous prison known as the Hanoi Hilton. The descriptions are unreal, unspeakable, beyond belief—and beyond human endurance.

Your bed is a cold cement slab in a six-foot-square cell. The smell of human excrement burns the nostrils. Rats the size of small cats run across the slab around you. The walls, floors and ceiling are caked with filth. Bars cover a tiny window high above the door. You are cold, hungry and aching from injuries. Months, even years, may go by without a glimpse of the sun, moon, grass or trees. All you can do is breathe the stale, rotten air and try to keep your sanity.

That's a little taste of what it was probably like for Joseph. How did he survive his prison? Well, he discovered a secret, one that the apostle Paul alludes to in Philippians 4:

> I know how to be brought low, and I know how to abound. In any and every circumstance, I have learned the secret of facing plenty and hunger, abundance and need. I can do all things through him who strengthens me. (4:12–13)

That's quite profound, but exactly what is the secret to the good life, the solution you and I desperately need to know? How do we cope when we are crying out in pain, struggling with anger, frustration, wanting to get even and asking, "Why is this happening to me? Why doesn't God help me out? Why doesn't anyone seem to care?" The secret is obvious, and it is simply this: stop asking "why" and start asking "what."

Joseph was a master at this. He did not ask "why." He refused to question God, his circumstances or even his brothers (as you'll see by the end of the book of Genesis). He kept asking "what"—"What can I do?"

When he was a slave, Joseph went to his master and said, "What do you want me to do?" In the prison, he went to the prison guard and asked, "How can I help you?" Maybe he said, "This place needs a good cleaning. Get me a mop and I'll clean it for you."

Joseph was a server, a man who set himself free from the prison of "why" by using the key of "what"—what do you need, how can I help, what can I do. That's the kind of guy that keeps getting elevated. As we read on, we see that they put Joseph in charge of the whole prison. This is what can happen to you if you stop asking "why" and start asking "what."

I'm a guy who has locked himself in the prison of "why" before. Maybe you've been there too. No one put you there, and no one can keep you there. You put yourself there, because you keep asking why—"Why did this happen to me? Why do I always get the short end of the stick? Why aren't things working out?" Joseph could have easily asked those questions, over and over. But instead of sitting in a corner whining about "why," he started asking "what."

When I learned to ask "what," it was the key that unlocked the door and set me free. Asking "why" put me in the prison, and the only thing that got me out was changing my "whys" to "whats."

Let's see how, in Genesis 40, Joseph began asking "what" and it really made a world of difference in his life. It's the secret to a good life, no matter what the circumstances. This is what the apostle Paul was talking about. "I learned the secret," he said, and the secret is serving—asking "what": What does the Lord want? What can I do? What should I do?

Serving the Downcast

While in prison, Joseph asked what he could do to help the downcast:

> Some time after this, the cupbearer of the king of Egypt and his baker committed an offense against their lord the king of Egypt. And Pharaoh was angry with his two officers, the chief cupbearer and the chief baker, and he put them in custody in the house of the captain of the guard, in the prison where Joseph was confined. The captain of the guard appointed Joseph to be with them, and he attended them. They continued for some time in custody. And one night they both dreamed—the cupbearer and the baker of the king of Egypt, who were confined in the prison—each his own dream, and each dream with its own interpretation. When Joseph came to them in the morning, he saw that they were troubled. So he asked Pharaoh's officers who were with him in custody in his master's house, "Why are your faces downcast today?" They said to him, "We have had dreams, and there is no one to interpret them." And Joseph said to them, "Do not interpretations belong to God? Please tell them to me." (Gen. 40:1–8)

It is interesting that Joseph takes notice of these two prisoners to such an extent that he can tell they are troubled by the look on their faces. A person who is asking "why" (as in "Why me?") is focused on himself, so he would never notice. But Joseph notices, because "what" focuses on others. Look at what Joseph says to them in verse 7: "Why are your faces downcast today?" (Yes, the question starts with "why," but it's clearly a "what" question: "What's wrong?")

I suppose they could have been annoyed by that question and responded, "Joe, have you noticed we're in prison? Why wouldn't we be sad?" But that's how different life is when you're not asking "why" but "what," and become focused on others. They could sense Joseph's genuine concern for them, so they told him they had no one to interpret their dreams. (They clearly believed that dreams had meaning and significance.)

"Interpretations are from the Lord," Joseph replied. "Only the Lord can tell you the truth about what's going on. Why don't you tell them to me?" He is suggesting that he might be able to help. He's acting as a counselor to these prisoners.

As a young Christian, I had several friends who had a huge impact on me. One taught me to share my faith; another showed me how to disciple others; another taught me how to counsel others; still another taught me how to pray for others. But I would have to say that what they all taught me was how to have a good life—the life of a servant. When you are into taking, it doesn't work out well. These friends taught me the same thing in different ways: how to serve others. It's no wonder I went into ministry—what could be more fulfilling than that?

Joseph understood the secret: stop asking "why." Why don't I have more stuff, why can't I have this, why don't I have a better job, why am I sick, why, why, why—stop it! Change that "why" to "what" and watch what happens to your life.

Serving the Lord

The second thing we learn from Joseph is to serve the Lord.

> So the chief cupbearer told his dream to Joseph and said to him, "In my dream there was a vine before me, and on the vine there were three branches. As soon it budded, its blossoms shot forth, and the clusters ripened into grapes. Pharaoh's cup was in my hand, and I took the grapes and

NO MATTER WHAT

> pressed them into Pharaoh's cup and placed the cup in
> Pharaoh's hand." Then Joseph said to him, "This is its in-
> terpretation: the three branches are three days. In three
> days Pharaoh will lift up your head and restore you to
> your office, and you shall place Pharaoh's cup in his hand
> as formerly, when you were his cupbearer. Only remember
> me when it is well with you, and please do me the kind-
> ness to mention me to Pharaoh, and so get me out of this
> house. For I was indeed stolen out of the land of the He-
> brews, and here also I have done nothing that they should
> put me into the pit. (Gen. 40:9–15)

Joseph's ability to interpret these dreams was supernatural; he said so himself: "Do not interpretations belong to
God?" People don't just know these things. You and I also
have supernatural gifts, given to us by God the day we become Christians. Let's look at First Corinthians 12, just one
list of spiritual gifts:

> Now there are varieties of gifts, but the same Spirit; and
> there are varieties of service, but the same Lord, and
> there are varieties of activities but it is the same God who
> empowers them all in everyone. To each is given the man-
> ifestation of the Spirit for the common good. For to one
> is given through the Spirit the utterance of wisdom, and
> to another the utterance of knowledge according to the
> same Spirit, to another faith by the same Spirit, to another
> gifts of healing by the one Spirit, to another the working
> of miracles, to another prophecy, to another the ability
> to distinguish between spirits, to another various kinds
> of tongues, to another the interpretation of tongues. All
> these are empowered by one and the same Spirit, who ap-
> portions to each one individually as he wills. (12:4–11)

"To each" means you and me. Everyone who is truly a
Christian in the church is given a spiritual gift. You have a gift

44

by the Holy Spirit. It's not your ability. It might be in accordance with your abilities, but it is over and beyond your abilities. It's a gift given by God. That's what we are reading about in this text. Joseph had an ability to interpret dreams, but he made it clear that it is God who gives the interpretation.

People have told me "Marty, you preached a great sermon. You really are a good public speaker." No, I'm not! If you had known me before I was a Christian, you would agree that this is not my ability. I was horrible at public speaking. What happened? Only one thing: I became a Christian. I was born again by the Holy Spirit. And the Spirit enables me to speak. He inspires me, shows me what to say and has taught me the Word of God.

It's the same with anyone's spiritual gift. Your gift might be serving, or helps, or something else, whether it's on this list or not. But I guarantee you, if you are really a Christian, you have a gift. And that is the key to serving the Lord. Like Joseph, you need to know your spiritual gift and use it.

When I preach, it's scary getting up in front of everybody, but God gives me such joy, such fulfillment! He wants to do the same with you, whether it's public speaking, or caring for kids, or helping people, or working with senior citizens, or teaching or counseling. There's a myriad of things that you can do. The question is, what are you doing? Are you just sitting there asking "why"? Or have you asked, "What am I supposed to do?"

I think one of the best ways to discover your spiritual gift is to just try different things, and suddenly you will start seeing your gift. I tried all kinds of different things before God brought me to the place of being able to speak. God has placed a particular hunger in you for something. Find it. Get into the action. God will show you what to do and will use your gift to work through you in a supernatural way.

I remember one time I was riding in a car with another guy and began witnessing to him. I asked him questions, and he asked me questions. I shared with him about how I became a Christian. He seemed a bit interested, so I kept talking with him. (I didn't know it at that time, but he wasn't telling me everything.)

Suddenly I had this overwhelming sense that this guy was going to become a Christian. I just knew it (probably like Joseph "just knew" the interpretation when the cupbearer told his dream). So I said him, "You know what? God's got your number, buddy. He's after you, pal. You're going to become a Christian, and soon."

Well, he didn't become a Christian that day. He didn't become a Christian for over two years. But then one day I got a phone call from him. He said, "I remembered those words you told me in the car that day. I just had to call you." What he didn't share with me that day in the car was that his marriage was falling apart. He had left his wife, had become hooked on drugs and was in a downward spiral.

Then he said, "I remembered those words you said in the car and God started speaking to me. Next thing I know, I'm back with my wife. We go to counseling and our marriage is healed. I get baptized in church. Now I'm leading a marriage ministry with my wife." He became a new creation in Christ—and God showed me that two years before!

God does that kind of thing now and then. Who knows how God will gift you? I even wonder sometimes if He doesn't gift us in different ways in different circumstances, in different situations with different people. You find yourself in a situation where you don't think you can do anything. But with the help of God, you can, because you quit asking "why" and asked "what"—"Lord, what can I do?" That's the key.

Serving the Truth

There's a third thing we can learn about serving from Joseph. Let's look a little further:

> When the chief baker saw that the interpretation was favorable, he said to Joseph, "I also had a dream: there were three cake baskets on my head, and in the uppermost basket there were all sorts of baked food for Pharaoh, but the birds were eating it out of the basket on my head." And Joseph answered and said, "This is its interpretation: the three baskets are three days. In three days Pharaoh will lift up your head—from you!—and hang you on a tree. And the birds will eat the flesh from you." (Gen. 40:16–19)

Can you imagine saying that to somebody? It's terrible! We may wonder why Joseph didn't soften it a bit or hedge in the interpretation. But he told the truth, even though it was a hard truth to tell. Why?

In his book *The Godward Life*, John Piper explains why being truth-driven is so crucial. He says that our concern with truth is an expression of our concern with God. He is the God of truth, and what He thinks about everything is what we should think about everything. In essence, Piper says, to not care about truth is to not care about God. If our ministries are God-centered, then logic dictates that our ministries must be truth-driven, because God is truth. The logic is flawless: what is not true is not of God and what is false is anti-God. You cannot minister in indifference because it would be indifference to the mind of God. Our concern with truth simply reflects our concern with God.[1]

So when we ask why Joseph told the truth and why we should be concerned about the truth, the answer is because the truth is of God. God does not live outside truth. If you have little concern for the truth, you can't be following God, because God only lives in truth. No wonder Joseph tells the truth. This is the kind of person he is. He's sold out to truth—he's not going to hedge the truth, put his own spin on it or speak half truths. So he tells the man the truth. And just as Joseph said, the dreams came true:

> On the third day, which was Pharaoh's birthday, he made a feast for all his servants and lifted up the head of the chief cupbearer and the head of the chief baker among his servants. He restored the chief cupbearer to his position, and he placed the cup in Pharaoh's hand. But he hanged the chief baker, as Joseph had interpreted to them. (Gen. 40:20–22)

Are you aware that dreams and their interpretation still happen in our day? It happened in my own neighborhood.

There was a couple who lived down the street from me for years, Barry and Cheryl Shaw. In fact, for a while Barry, an attorney, was the mayor of our township. He was Jewish and wouldn't even say the word "Jesus." My wife and I would run into them sometimes when we were out for a walk, and we would stop and have a little neighborly conversation, not knowing what was going on in their lives.

Barry had become very frustrated with Jewish traditions and was starting to look into New Age teachings. One day, he had an amazing dream in which he saw Jesus hanging on the cross. And he said to himself, even in the midst of the dream, "Why am I seeing Jesus? I don't believe in Him." He came to me later and told me about it.

Then Cheryl had a similar dream, in which an angel told her that she needed to follow Jesus! They started listening to Christian radio and heard me preach. They eventually ended up coming to our church and became Christians, as did their daughter and her husband, their son and his wife, and her parents—who were in their 80s! And it all started with dreams. This is not that uncommon an experience for Jewish people. It is not that uncommon for people in the Muslim tradition, either. They have dreams, and it wakes them up to reality.

Have you found the secret to a good life? Have you stopped asking "why" and started asking "what"? That's the kind of life Joseph had—no matter what the circumstance, he seems to have found a way to be set free, even though he was in prison, by simply asking, "What does the Lord want me to do? What are the needs of others?" You've got the key—just unlock the door!

It's easy to go to church and just be a consumer. If your church is anything like mine, there are probably a lot of ministries where you and your family can receive help, counseling, teaching, training, etc. There's nothing wrong with that. But if that's all you're doing, that's not a good life. A good life begins when you start serving others and using the spiritual gift God's given you. That's where true joy and freedom are, when you stop asking "why" and start asking "what."

Unfortunately for Joseph, chapter 40 ends on a sad note: "Yet the chief cupbearer did not remember Joseph, but forgot him" (Gen. 40:23). That's the end of the chapter, but not the end of the story, as we'll see soon.

Prayer

Lord, I come before you to give thanks for all you have taught me in this story—the lesson of "why" and "what." So often I get stuck in the "whys," Lord, and I need to stop. I ask you to help me learn to say "what" instead of "why." What do You want me to do? What can I do to serve others? How can I help the downcast? How can I serve the Lord in this situation? I want to serve You, Lord. That is what you gifted me for. No more "whys," only You, Lord, and the question of "what." In Jesus' name, Amen.

Chapter 4

GOD IS CALLING

Genesis 41

Marty Berglund

God calls you to take a stand.

Before we begin chapter 41 of Genesis, let's recap what we've learned so far about Joseph and what kind of man he was. Sometimes to get a picture of what someone is like, it helps to look at the polar opposite—what they are not like. So here are some characteristics describing what Joseph is not.

- *Wishy-washy*: Does this describe Joseph? Not at all. Throughout his story, he has made some very clear decisions. He doesn't say one thing and do another. He's definitely not wishy-washy.
- *Cowardly*: Was Joseph a coward? There is no evidence of that in the story we've read so far. He seems very brave, in fact.
- *Resentful*: He was betrayed by his brothers, framed by Potiphar's wife, ends up in prison and is forgotten by

the cupbearer. Is there one word in what we've read about his resentment? Not even a word!

- *Self-absorbed*: No. He tried to help the cupbearer and the baker. He tried to help anyone he could—and he was a slave! No, he is not self-absorbed.

In contrast, what are some descriptive terms that tell us what Joseph is like?

- *Very bold*: He doesn't seem to be afraid of anything or anybody. Whether in the presence of a king or his slave master, Potiphar, he's bold.
- *Stable*: He seems to have unbelievable stability. And I think we'll find that's because of the stand he took for the Lord.
- *Clear-thinking*: He's able to interpret dreams that no one else can figure out. He's able to see things other people can't see. He's very clear-thinking.
- *Leader*: He's very much a leader—a servant leader. Whether he's literally a servant or serving in the jail, he just seems to want to help. He's always asking, "What can I do? How can I help?" He wants to serve. We talked about that in the last chapter.

I want to suggest that people with these kinds of characteristics are those who have taken a stand for the Lord—hence the title of this chapter. There are several places in the life of Joseph where you can plainly see he took a stand.

When he has conflict with his brothers, he stands his ground, following the Lord. When he is tempted by Potiphar's wife to have a sexual affair (which he probably could have gotten away with) he won't do it because he has taken a stand. He works hard for those over him, even though it doesn't always end well.

Joseph took a stand when he was young. It was not natural for him; it was hard. But Joseph was a person who was willing to take a stand, no matter what. And the things that happened in his life happened because he took a stand.

Taking a stand is something many of us have done: a stand for your rights as an American citizen, a stand as a captain of a team or something like that. But what I'm talking about is taking a stand for the Lord.

This kid, at seventeen years old, took a strong stand and held to it, no matter what happened to him. No matter what people did to him or said to him or the consequences or circumstances he was in, he believed and took a stand, knowing that the Lord was with him and was going to work it out. We are going to see the amazing results of this in chapter 41.

But first let's look at Ephesians 6, where the apostle Paul tells us to take a stand with the whole armor of God, a listing of character qualities needed to do spiritual battle:

> Therefore take up the whole armor of God, that you may be able to withstand in the evil day, and having done all, to stand firm. Stand therefore, having fastened on the belt of truth, and having put on the breastplate of righteousness. (6:13–14)

Paul is saying that we have been given this whole armor of God—all these great truths, all the righteousness given to us in Christ, all the benefits we have as Christians—so that we can "stand firm," or take a stand.

People who only take a stand for themselves, for what they want and what they can get, are wimps. History doesn't say much about people like that. People who take a stand for something bigger than themselves are the ones we read about in the history books. They are like Joseph! They stand firmly for something and truth is magnified through their lives.

I don't know about you, but that's the kind of person I want to be. I want to be a person who makes a difference, a true follower of Jesus. You and I can do that, and we can learn how by looking at Joseph.

God Calls You to Stand and Wait for the Lord

The first thing we learn about Joseph in chapter 41 is this: he had to wait. When you take a stand for the Lord, sometimes the Lord will call you to then wait on Him.

> After two whole years, Pharaoh dreamed that he was standing by the Nile, and behold, there came up out of the Nile seven cows attractive and plump, and they fed in the reed grass. And behold, seven other cows, ugly and thin, came up out of the Nile after them, and stood by the other cows on the bank of the Nile. And the ugly, thin cows ate up the seven attractive, plump cows. And Pharaoh awoke. And he fell asleep and dreamed a second time. And behold, seven ears of grain, plump and good, were growing on one stalk. And behold, after them sprouted seven ears, thin and blighted by the east wind. And the thin ears swallowed up the seven plump, full ears. And Pharaoh awoke, and behold, it was a dream. So in the morning his spirit was troubled, and he sent and called for all the magicians of Egypt and all its wise men. Pharaoh told them his dreams, but there was none who could interpret them to Pharaoh. Then the chief cupbearer said to Pharaoh, "I remember my offenses today. When Pharaoh was angry with his servants and put me and the chief baker in custody, in the house of the captain of the guard, we dreamed

on the same night, he and I, each having a dream with its own interpretation. A young Hebrew was there with us, a servant of the captain of the guard. When we told him, he interpreted our dreams to us, giving an interpretation to each man according to his dream. And as he interpreted to us, so it came about. I was restored to my office, and the baker was hanged.

Then Pharaoh sent and called Joseph, and they quickly brought him out of the pit. And when he had shaved himself and changed his clothes, he came in before Pharaoh. And Pharaoh said to Joseph, "I have had a dream and there is no one who can interpret it. I have heard it said of you that when you hear a dream you can interpret it." Joseph answered Pharaoh, "It is not in me; God will give Pharaoh a favorable answer." (Gen. 41:1–16)

Joseph had to wait two full years for the cupbearer to remember to speak up for him. As we read further in the passage, we will see he is thirty years old at this point, so it's been about thirteen years since he first took his stand, since he was sold into slavery by his brothers. So, in total, he's been waiting for *thirteen* years! But he was still believing in the Lord. He took a stand that the Lord was going to care for him.

Sometimes the Lord will call you and me to take a stand and wait. Maybe you are still waiting. Sometimes the waiting may last almost a lifetime. In modern American culture, we like fast Internet, fast phones, fast food. We like fast—waiting is just unacceptable. But in the Bible, waiting is something that's held in high esteem. For example, look at Psalm 27:14:

Wait for the Lord; be strong, and let your heart take courage; wait for the Lord!

Or consider Isaiah 40:31:

> But they who wait for the Lord shall renew their strength;
> they shall mount up with wings like eagles; they shall run
> and not be weary; they shall walk and not faint.

Did you notice the key word is "wait"? Let's look at another one, this time from the New Testament:

> And while staying with them he ordered them not to depart from Jerusalem, but to wait for the promise of the Father, which, he said, "you heard from me." (Acts 1:4)

This is Jesus talking about the promise of the Holy Spirit, *before* the day of Pentecost in Acts 2. What did they have to do for the power of the Holy Spirit to come upon them—the power that made them into bold witnesses for Christ? They had to wait in the upper room.

There are other passages we could look at that talk about waiting, but this question remains: why? Why, when you take a stand for the Lord, does God make you wait? The answer is in verse 16 of Genesis 41. Pharaoh says to Joseph, "I understand you know how to interpret dreams." And his response is, "It is not in me."

That's the answer! "It's not in me." If you are going to take a stand and really be used by the Lord, if you're really going to find strength in the Lord, you have to wait—because you don't have it! Joseph is basically saying to Pharaoh, "It's very flattering that you think I've got the interpretation, but I don't. I have to wait on the Lord. Only the Lord has it."

That's what it really means to take a stand for the Lord. It means waiting for the Lord to show up—waiting for the Lord to guide you, waiting for the Lord to teach you. That is what God does in a period of waiting—He works on your character, teaches you some lessons, helps you gain a perspective you didn't have before. This is why the Bible takes waiting and elevates it. Wait on the Lord and you'll mount up with wings like eagles.

Albert Benjamin Simpson, the founder of the Christian and Missionary Alliance, had an entire theology of waiting. He said that God uses seasons of waiting to make great spiritual transitions. Through them, we are led to new planes and new advances. Sometimes we have to make a complete break to get out of our old ruts and be free to go higher and become bolder.

Simpson said that the wisest thing to do before a season of blessing is to take an inventory, not of our riches but of our poverty. He said we need to count all the voids and vacuums and places of insufficiency. Using a farming illustration, he said we need to dig ditches, bring them to God to fill them and then wait for the harvest. God will search the depths of our being and show us our folly, failures and needs. Like growing a good crop, there are spiritual conditions that just can't be accomplished in a moment. We need to break up the fallow ground, have the frosts of winter and the rains of spring to prepare the soil.

And still, sometimes, nothing happens for days and days. At least we don't see it happening. But the dry ground that is our heart is slowly absorbing the water until it is ready. And when the waiting is done, we will know that all the work and all the waiting was not in vain.

Simpson said that we just don't wait enough upon the Lord or spend enough time at the mercy seat. We rush, we hurry, our schedules are so busy and we lose time instead of gaining it. We have to wait upon the Lord.[1]

Simpson said this over a hundred years ago, but it is even more true today. Our schedules are busy and we can't seem to be patient. We've got to learn to wait on the Lord, to take a solid stand and refuse to do anything until the Lord tells us to move. Joseph was that kind of person—whether in jail or in slavery, betrayed or tempted, he waited for the Lord.

God Calls You to Stand and Look for the Lord

Pharaoh recounts the dream to Joseph, and he responds:

> Then Joseph said to Pharaoh, "The dreams of Pharaoh are one; God has revealed to Pharaoh what he is about to do. The seven good cows are seven years, and the seven good ears are seven years; the dreams are one. The seven lean and ugly cows that came up after them are seven years, and the seven empty ears blighted by the east wind are also seven years of famine. It is as I told Pharaoh; God has shown to Pharaoh what he is about to do. There will come seven years of great plenty throughout all the land of Egypt, but after them there will arise seven years of famine, and all the plenty will be forgotten in the land of Egypt. The famine will consume the land, and the plenty will be unknown in the land by reason of the famine that will follow, for it will be very severe. And the doubling of Pharaoh's dream means that the thing is fixed by God, and God will shortly bring it about. Now therefore let Pharaoh select a discerning and wise man, and set him over the land of Egypt. Let Pharaoh proceed to appoint overseers over the land and take one-fifth of the produce of the land of Egypt during the seven plentiful years. And let them gather all the food of these good years that are coming and store up grain under the authority of Pharaoh for food in the cities, and let them keep it. That food shall be a reserve for the land against the seven years of

> famine that are to occur in the land of Egypt, so that the land may not perish through the famine." (Gen. 41:25–36)

Can you imagine Pharaoh, this proud king, admitting that he has a problem, that he needs help? But he realized he couldn't identify the problem and get the right solution until he could get a correct interpretation.

We are in the same boat today. If you've got a problem, you're just like Pharaoh. You have to go to somebody who can give you the correct interpretation. All the wise men couldn't give it. But this little Hebrew guy, Joseph, gives Pharaoh a correct interpretation.

Notice that Joseph begins by saying, "God has revealed to Pharaoh what he is about to do." The correct interpretation needs to come from the Lord. We are not just psychological beings or physical beings; we are spiritual beings. We need to know God's interpretation of our circumstances, because we can't get the right answer if we don't identify the right problem.

Many people spend years trying to fix things in their lives, but they never get the right interpretation, so they never come up with the right solution. They just keep going around in circles, not getting anywhere. Do you know anyone like that? Does that describe you?

The only reason the story of Joseph is of any value to us today is because in this ancient literature, preserved over thousands of years, we find the record of a person who has heard from God. Joseph told Pharaoh that God reveals things to human beings.

This is just one instance in a whole book of records and evidence showing how God reveals things to us. The evidence can be found from Genesis through Revelation. In story after story, miracle after miracle, testimony after testimony, is the record that God reveals things to people. And He still does today. Are you looking for Him to speak to your need, or are you leaving God out? In light of all the evidence, we should be looking for God to reveal things to us.

God Calls You to Stand and Lead for the Lord

Let's read to the end of the chapter.

> This proposal pleased Pharaoh and all his servants. And Pharaoh said to his servants, "Can we find a man like this, in whom is the Spirit of God?" Then Pharaoh said to Joseph, "Since God has shown you all this, there is none so discerning and wise as you are. You shall be over my house, and all my people shall order themselves as you command. Only as regards the throne will I be greater than you."
>
> And Pharaoh said to Joseph, "See, I have set you over all the land of Egypt." Then Pharaoh took his signet ring from his hand and put it on Joseph's hand, and clothed him in garments of fine linen and put a gold chain about his neck. And he made him ride in his second chariot. And they called out before him, "Bow the knee!" Thus he set him over all the land of Egypt. Moreover, Pharaoh said to Joseph, "I am Pharaoh, and without your consent no one shall lift up hand or foot in all the land of Egypt." And Pharaoh called Joseph's name Zaphenath-paneah. And he gave him in marriage Asenath, the daughter of Potiphera priest of On. So Joseph went out over the land of Egypt. Joseph was thirty years old when he entered the service of Pharaoh king of Egypt. And Joseph went out from the presence of Pharaoh and went through all the land of Egypt. During the seven plentiful years the earth produced abundantly, and he gathered up all the food of these

seven years, which occurred in the land of Egypt, and put the food in the cities. He put in every city the food from the fields around it. And Joseph stored up grain in great abundance, like the sand of the sea, until he ceased to measure it, for it could not be measured.

Before the year of famine came, two sons were born to Joseph. Asenath, the daughter of Potiphera priest of On, bore them to him. Joseph called the name of the firstborn Manasseh, "For," he said, "God has made me forget all my hardship and all my father's house." The name of the second he called Ephraim, "For God has made me fruitful in the land of my affliction."

The seven years of plenty that occurred in the land of Egypt came to an end, and the seven years of famine began to come, as Joseph had said. There was famine in all lands, but in all the land of Egypt there was bread. When all the land of Egypt was famished, the people cried to Pharaoh for bread. Pharaoh said to all the Egyptians, "Go to Joseph. What he says to you, do."

So when the famine had spread over all the land, Joseph opened all the storehouses and sold to the Egyptians, for the famine was severe in the land of Egypt. Moreover, all the earth came to Egypt to Joseph to buy grain, because the famine was severe over all the earth. (Gen. 41:37–57)

What a turnaround for Joseph! To be appointed prime minister at the age of thirty is pretty significant, especially considering the route he took to get there. Pharaoh gave Joseph his signet ring. That was the ancient equivalent of pulling out his Platinum Visa card and saying, "Anything you need, you can have it. Just put it on the card."

The historical record tells us that other countries came to Egypt and offered land, riches and loyalty in exchange for grain. Egypt became the most powerful nation in the world, all because Joseph correctly interpreted the dream of Pharaoh and set up a system to store grain.

Joseph was exalted because he took a stand. Those who stand out in history are those who take a stand. Your life and your legacy will be determined by what kind of a stand you take. If your stand is just for yourself, for what you can get and for your rights, you probably won't be recognized much at all because that's totally normal and natural. But if you take a stand for something bigger than yourself, if you take a stand for the Lord, you'll have a legacy. These are the kind of people who make a difference.

On the personal side, Joseph had two sons and he named the first son Manasseh ("causing to forget"), "For," he said "God has made me forget all my hardship and all my father's house." Joseph took a stand for the Lord and it changed his life. He was able to forget all his hardships. Do you have hardships you can't forget, things that haunt you still—the guilt, the shame, the sorrow, the grief? The answer is to take a stand for the Lord. It's how you move on in life.

He named his next son Ephraim ("fruitful"), "for God has made me fruitful in the land of my affliction." Often we look at our affliction as something we can't believe is happening to us, something we can't get over. Joseph took a stand for the Lord and became fruitful even in his affliction. Isn't that what we all desire—that there is some kind of fruit from our affliction, that it has some kind of purpose and meaning? It will if you take a stand for the Lord.

Can you imagine what would happen if the people in your local church took a stand for the Lord in the areas of finances, morality, marriage, profession? You watch what God will do. You will see meaning and purpose in your life like you never had before because you took a stand.

The apostle Paul said, "For if we live, we live to the Lord, and if we die, we die to the Lord. So then, whether we live or whether we die, we are the Lord's" (Romans 14:8). Why do we read about the apostle Paul? Because he took a stand! Why do we read about Joseph? Because he took a stand! Will anybody talk about you after you're gone? Will your grand-children remember what kind of a stand you took? Will you take a stand for the Lord?

Prayer

Lord, I need this kind of challenge. And I need Your power and strength to help me meet it. I'm counting on You, Lord. From this moment on, I'm standing for the Lord. That's what my life is all about. I want to take a stand for You, Lord, and make a difference in my world. And some day when I go to heaven, I know I won't regret a single minute that I stood for the Lord. In Jesus' name, Amen.

Chapter 5

CHANGES FOR GOOD

Genesis 42 & 43

Marty Berglund

Insights that can bring changes for good into your life.

We now arrive at one of the most dramatic scenes in the entire Bible. Books, plays and even a musical have been written about it. Scholars have studied it. And there is good reason for it, because unbelievable insights about life await us in this story—insights that can literally change your life.

This long narrative covers all of Genesis 42 and 43, so rather than print the two chapters here in their entirety I suggest you get your Bible, read these chapters and keep your Bible at your elbow as we go through our discussion.

As you read Genesis 42 and 43, do you sense the tension in this part of the story? Joseph's family arrives in Egypt. They don't know who he is but he recognizes them. The tension is so thick you can cut it with a knife. Let's look at three insights we can gather from this story.

Don't Let Fear Dominate You

Fear is the dominating influence in this passage. Fear is in control of everyone—Joseph and all his brothers.

Joseph has now been prime minister of Egypt for seven years, which means he has been away from home for twenty years. The last time his brothers saw him, he was a seventeen-year-old kid. But now he's dressed in an expensive robe, with his head shaved like an Egyptian, perhaps with a headdress and face paint. He is totally unrecognizable.

As people from various countries line up at the money changers' table to buy food, Joseph's brothers also arrive from Canaan. Can you imagine Joseph's reaction when his brothers, all ten of them, walk in the door? They're a little older, a little balder maybe, but there they are!

He gasps when he sees them; his heart starts beating rapidly; he turns around and walks away. He thinks, "What should I do? Will they know who I am?" So he walks back out again and notices that they don't recognize him. He says to himself, "How do I handle this? I know! I'll accuse them of spying on Egypt!"

Joseph steps up and says "Hey, you ten guys, come over here! I want to talk to you right now! I know what you're up to. You are checking us out so you can rob us. That's what you're here for."

"No, no, we wouldn't do that! We're all from one family and we're just here to get—"

"I don't believe a word you're saying. You know what? I'm going to throw you in jail." He probably did that just to buy some time to think about what to do.

Have you noticed that all of them are operating on fear? Joseph's afraid of them, and they're afraid of him. When they are sent back home, they're afraid of their dad, and their dad's afraid as well. There is a lot of emotion in this story, and the major one is fear.

Fear is not always a bad emotion; it's not always wrong. But when it dominates your life, it's wrong. At some time in your life you have probably experienced fear wrapping itself around you until you can hardly move, you can hardly think. Ever have a sleepless night, dominated by fear? Everyone in this story is afraid—afraid of God, of each other, of their circumstances, of their future. They are afraid of everything. Look at some of the references to fear in this passage:

> And Reuben answered them, "Did I not tell you not to sin against the boy? But you did not listen. So now there comes a reckoning for his blood." (Gen. 42:22)

Doesn't that sound like a big brother? I had a big brother, so I know. They are always quick to point out, "You should have listened to me." He's afraid of God's judgment: "We're getting paid back for what we did." Everything is going on here—guilt, fear, everything!

> Then he turned away from them and wept. And he returned to them and spoke to them. And he took Simeon from them and bound him before their eyes. (42:24)

What's going on here? Fear! Joseph is afraid (at this point, though his heart is breaking, he's apparently still afraid to reveal who he is). And the brothers, of course, are afraid. Fear is just dominating.

> He said to his brothers, "My money has been put back; here it is in the mouth of my sack!" At this their hearts failed

them, and they turned trembling to one another, saying, "What is this that God has done to us?" (Gen. 42:28)

"Trembling"—that's fear, isn't it? Now they are even afraid of what God is giving them because of what they did.

As they emptied their sacks, behold, every man's bundle of money was in his sack. And when they and their father saw their bundles of money, they were afraid. (42:35)

It just outright says they were afraid!

But he said, "My son shall not go down with you, for his brother is dead, and he is the only one left. If harm should happen to him on the journey that you are to make, you would bring down my gray hairs with sorrow to Sheol." (42:38)

Jacob thinks Joseph is dead. Benjamin is the only one left of Rachel's two boys. He's afraid the grief will kill him if Benjamin gets killed.

And the men were afraid because they were brought to Joseph's house, and they said, "It is because of the money, which was replaced in our sacks the first time, that we are brought in, so that he may assault us and fall upon us to make us servants and seize our donkeys." (43:18)

Everybody is afraid of everything—even when Joseph treats them with kindness and holds a feast for them at his house, it causes them to fear. Sometimes this is what happens when tension is building in a family—fear dominates everything.

At a monthly meeting of area pastors, where we pray for each other, talk with each other and keep each other up to speed, we were studying together in Romans 8. The beginning of that chapter is all about the Holy Spirit.

I asked all these pastors, "If you could use just one word to describe how you know that God is working in your life, that the Holy Spirit is there, what word would you use?" They were thinking about it. One or two pastors shared. And this one pastor began to share. As soon as he opened his mouth, you could tell he was getting choked up.

He said, "Two years ago, I couldn't have answered that question. I just couldn't feel it, I couldn't sense it. All my life I've felt like I didn't quite measure up. If people told me how good my sermon was, I'd say 'Yes, but I should have said this or that.' I got almost all As in school but never felt I was good enough. But two years ago, everything changed."

He said, "I began to understand more clearly the mercy of God, the grace of God. There is just one word and that word is 'worth.' Now for the first time in my life, after all the seminary training, all the years of being a pastor, I am finally realizing, I was worth it—to God! That's the only conclusion I can come to. That's the only thing the grace of God can mean. That's the only reason that Jesus would die on the cross. I'm worth it!"

By this time he was crying and got most of us crying along with him. He said, "I was worth it. I can't believe I'm worth it!" All the fear that dominated him that he'd never measure up was erased when he started to realize the grace of God: "I'm worth it."

And that's where the fear came from in Joseph's family. No one really comprehended the grace of God. You're worth it. God's grace is toward you. Joseph begins to get it, and eventually, you will see that it spreads through the whole family.

Not one of Joseph's brothers truly understood that God would protect them and provide for them, because they didn't understand that God sees them as worth it. These men were the patriarchs of the twelve tribes of Israel—though, of course, they don't know that yet. But God thinks they are worth it.

How about you? Do you not know how "worth it" you are to God? That's what takes fear away. I'm reminded of a passage in First John: "There is no fear in love, but perfect love casts out fear. For fear has to do with punishment, and whoever fears has not been perfected in love" (4:18).

Faith Can Overcome Dysfunction

This is a very dysfunctional family. The fact that they sold their brother as a slave was probably one sign of dysfunction. Another sign might be that when their sister was raped, they went over to the neighbors who raped her and killed a bunch of random people. And yet, in the midst of the dysfunction, there is one man, Joseph, who believes God—no matter what. And because of that, the whole family is altered, changed, redeemed. Isn't that amazing?

> On the third day Joseph said to them, "Do this and you will live, for I fear God." (Gen. 42:18)

Now Joseph introduces a new kind of fear—the fear that comes from faith. "I fear God. I fear Yahweh. Therefore, I'm not afraid of you, your father, the circumstances or Egypt." What that word means is "I revere Him. I respect Him. I honor Him. I have faith in Him." And this is how Joseph introduces all that he's going to say: "I fear God."

By now, though, you are probably wondering what kind of game he's playing. He's putting money in their sacks and sending them away to be caught. Scholars have debated this. Some have suggested that he's using his authority to intimidate, to give them a little payback. Others think that maybe he's heaping pain and terror upon them like they did upon him or is playing a kind of cat-and-mouse game.

But the vast majority of scholars recognize that there is no indication of anything like that in the passage. What's really going on is that Joseph is trying to buy time, trying to figure out what to do to bring this family back together.

> He [Joseph's steward] replied, "Peace to you, do not be afraid. Your God and the God of your father has put treasure in your sacks for you. I received your money." Then he brought Simeon out to them. (Gen. 43:23)

Notice that the steward, who works for Joseph, didn't say, "The boss told us to put money in your sacks." He said, "God put money in your sack." Where does he get this idea about God from? From Joseph! When one person believes, it infects other people. He knew how the money got in the sack, but he also knew that God told Joseph to do it.

Here are the people who will become the twelve tribes of Israel, yet at least ten of them are behaving like unbelievers! They are rebuked by the steward, who, in essence, says, "Trust God. What's your problem?" It's like a pagan saying to a Christian, "Don't you believe God? I thought you were a Christian." The steward obviously got the idea from the one person in the story who really fears God—Joseph—right in the midst of all the dysfunction.

As a pastor for over thirty years, I have seen a lot of dysfunction—a lot. Some of the people in my church have gone through tremendous dysfunction. When Joseph weeps in this story, they can relate, because they either came from a dysfunctional family or are still in one. I've heard countless stories about physical and sexual abuse. One guy shared about being beaten many times by his dad and knocked out cold at least three times. Others have been cheated out of their inheritances by a brother or sister.

I've heard people say they haven't talked to a brother, child or other relative for fifteen or twenty years. Others have told me that they never really knew their dad because he was always gone or that their mother told them she wished they had never been born. Foster kids have shared about being raised in a system rampant with abuse. And the list goes on: abortions, emotional cruelty, divorce, crime, drugs, alcohol, rape—some things so horrific people won't even tell you about them.

I say this because you need to see in this story what happens when one man believes God will take care of him in the midst of the dysfunction. I'm challenging you, if any of this sounds like your own family, can you be a Joseph? Can you say, "I don't care how bad it gets, I don't care how screwed up my family is, I'm believing God is going to work through it and bring redemption in the midst of all this heartache, pain and sin." That's what this story is all about. When one person can believe in the midst of dysfunction, God can do amazing things!

Trust God to Work in Amazing Ways

> When Jacob learned that there was grain for sale in Egypt, he said to his sons, "Why do you look at one another?" (Gen. 42:1)

Maybe it's because I was raised by a guy who was in the Marine Corps, but I can just hear Dad saying, "Why are you standing there looking at each other? There's food in Egypt. Go up to Egypt and get the food!" It's so funny—they're standing around looking at each other at the beginning of chapter 42, and if you look at the second to last verse in chapter 43, they are looking at each other again!

> And they sat before him, the firstborn according to his birthright and the youngest according to his youth. And the men looked at one another in amazement. (Gen. 43:33)

Joseph prepares a feast for everyone and seats them according to their ages, which really puzzles them. *How does this "stranger" know our ages?* But just as amazing is the food they are stuffing their faces with. They've got meat, cheese, dried fruit, nuts—all different kinds of food. They probably haven't had meat for weeks, months, years maybe. They are making faces at each other across the table, sitting there in absolute amazement, totally blessed, with money in their pockets that they thought they had spent. They don't know what in the world is going on—and this is just the beginning of the blessing that is going to come upon them. Instead of revenge, instead of trying to prove something, Joseph held out his heart to his sick, messed up, dysfunctional brothers. He had love in his heart.

It reminds me of Romans 5:5—"and hope does not put us to shame, because God's love has been poured into our hearts through the Holy Spirit who has been given to us." If you have been given the Holy Spirit by God, which is what happens when you become born again, you have a love in your heart that you didn't put there. God put it there. And this is what's happening to Joseph. He's got love for his brothers. It's unbelievable.

God took hold of one person in this dysfunctional family. How did that happen? That one person said, "God, I give you my life. Even if I'm a slave or a prisoner, I give you my heart." When that happens, you can overcome the fear and dysfunction and see what God can do, even in your family. But it starts when you give your heart and your life to the Lord.

I'm challenging you to be a Joseph.

Prayer

Lord, I give You my heart and my life. I believe You can and will take care of me no matter what. And I believe You will put love in my heart even for the dysfunctional people in my family that I don't love. You will give me love. You will pour Your love into me so that I can love others. I know that You will take care of me, no matter how much fear I have. I know You can handle it because perfect love casts out fear. I know You are going to do something really amazing through me if I give my heart and my life to You. Lord, they are Yours. In the name of Jesus Christ. Amen.

Chapter 6

CHANGES

Genesis 44

Don Hay

God wants to change you.

When was the last time you really had to wrestle through change? Not someone else changing (we can always come up with someone else we wish would change), but you, personally? When was the last time you had to really wrestle through what it would be like for you to change?

One of the times that came to mind as I tried to think through that question for myself was when I first got married. I've been married for fourteen years, and I learned very quickly that change was necessary. In the very beginning, I thought that all the change needed to happen on my wife's end—like a lot of husbands, I'm sure! She needed to be more patient, more understanding, less uptight, less stressed out, less sensitive.

But what I began to understand is that for our marriage to be healthy and to go the distance, I couldn't put all the weight on her; I had to change myself. And I really had to wrestle with what change looked like for me. I discovered in those early days just how selfish I was. I wasn't a bad guy— I just looked at everything through the lens of what made sense to me, instead of really thinking through how I could serve her. And so, through trial and error, I learned the simple truth that growth requires change, and change is hard.

Over the years as a pastor, I've seen it time and time again, in all kinds of relationships: marriage, dating, children and parents, friendships—it only takes one person who refuses to change to sabotage the relationship. You've probably been there; maybe you were the one who decided not to change. But change is necessary for growth and health.

Not all change is good; if you start lying when you used to be truthful, or you leave your spouse, or you start drinking heavily, that may be a change, but it's not a good one! I am talking about change that makes us grow. And many Christians do not seem to realize that change is also required if we want to grow spiritually.

I know, of course, that I change as I grow physically. When I was born, I depended on my parents for everything. But I began to grow and became more independent, until eventually I got a job and moved out of the house. We understand in earthly terms that as we grow, we change. That's life.

The same is true in our relationship with Christ. When we first come to faith, we start out as infants, dependent on others to tell us who God is. But as we grow, we become more independent, able to go directly to Him because our relationship with Christ matures. We change, we develop, we begin to have that one-on-one interaction with Him that we need.

We can all understand that who I was five years ago isn't who I should be five years from now, because I'm going to grow. The same is true spiritually—that is, unless we stick our heels in the ground and say, "God, I'm done. I don't want to grow anymore." If you don't want to change, then you don't want to grow.

Because God wants you to grow, God also wants you to change. Some people don't really come to grips with that. The New Testament is full of examples of Jesus meeting people and urging them to grow, to follow Him, to change. As a result, those He met changed dramatically—changed their direction, their behavior, their heart's desire.

In Matthew 4:19, Jesus calls Peter and Andrew to be His disciples, saying to them, "Follow me, and I will make you fishers of men." He was saying, "Follow me and I will change you. I will give your life new purpose."

Again, in John 3:3, Jesus says to Nicodemus, "Truly, truly, I say to you, unless one is born again, he cannot see the kingdom of God." Nicodemus can't figure out what He means by "born again," but Jesus is simply saying, "You must allow the Spirit to get inside you and change you, to remake you into something new."

We see it again in Luke 19:5. Jesus is coming through town and He sees Zacchaeus, a short little guy whom no one likes because he steals their money under the guise of collecting taxes: "And when Jesus came to the place, he looked up and said to him, 'Zacchaeus, hurry and come down, for I must stay at your house today.'" Jesus engages Zacchaeus, encouraging him to change, and he does. He stops ripping people off. Zacchaeus has a total life change.

The last verse we'll look at is Mark 10:21. A rich young man has just asked Jesus, "What do I need to do to be saved? I've done this, this, this and this. What's left? What else do I need to do?" In this verse, Jesus replies, "You lack one thing: go, sell all that you have and give to the poor, and you will have treasure in heaven; and come, follow me."

Jesus was saying, "You want to follow Me? You've got to change; you've got to grow. You've got to grow past your wealth and past identifying yourself by all the stuff you have. You need to sell it all because it's keeping you from knowing Me." Unfortunately, that much change was too much for the young man, and he went away sad—sad and unchanged.

These are just a few examples of Jesus engaging people in love and grace, but calling them to grow past where they are—and growth always involves change.

So what's the point? God wants you to grow. That's the reason you're reading this book. No matter why you think you ended up here in chapter 6, no matter what you're going to do when you put this book down, God wants you to grow. The reality is that if you and I commit to really following Jesus, something has to change. And ignoring this fact is one of the greatest downfalls of contemporary Christianity.

One of the greatest struggles that our generation faces in Christianity is that we pray to receive Christ but we never really change. We've taken an Almighty God, Creator of all things, who sent His Son to die on a cross and be raised for our justification, and we've turned Him into our private Savior that we tuck away and pull out when no one's around. We still look the same as everybody else; we haven't changed.

We realize that in the physical realm nothing can or should stay the way it is forever; things should be growing and changing. But spiritually, we've put our heels in the ground and said, "God, I'll let you change me this much, but not that much." Because we are not willing to change, we are radically missing out on a whole component of what it means to follow Jesus.

Instead of reducing your role in the Christian life to just praying a prayer, continuing to live as you have been and hoping that you're going to be blessed, I want you to ask yourself a question: "What does God want to change about me?" Not whom or what does He want to change *around* you—that's an easy question. What does He want to change about *you*? Have you really thought about that?

One of the primary functions of the Holy Spirit, according to John 16, is to illuminate our hearts and to reveal where real change needs to happen. Are you letting God do that? In your heart, your mind, your relationships, your thoughts, your behaviors, your dreams, your fears, your *life*? Are you asking God to change you, to renew your mind and conform you into the image of Jesus?

Let's get really specific about this. Grab a pen and write on the bottom of this page,

"God, I am ready for you to change _____."

Don't fill it in yet—just let it soak. My prayer is that, by the end of this chapter, God's Spirit will help you fill in that blank.

Wasn't that just the longest introduction ever? Now, let's look at Genesis 44 as we continue with the story of Joseph.

Change Hurts

We have been studying Joseph in these past few chapters, but chapter 44 is different. It has less to do with Joseph and a whole lot more to do with his brothers. Look back over the choices that his brothers made: they chose to hate Joseph, to sell him to slave traders, to fake his death and to stand there and not say a word while their father wept and grieved for Joseph. Now twenty years have gone by, yet it still feels like the middle of the story. (chapter 45 is the climax, with so much of an emotional release and so many things resolved. It is sort of the happy ending. I don't want to steal the thunder from the next chapter, but it's really one of the best passages in the Bible.)

But chapter 44 is the hinge point for the whole story. It is about the change that has to take place in the brothers, particularly Judah. Judah was the one who said, "Hey, why kill Joseph when we can sell him and make a profit?" I don't know if that makes him a good guy or a bad guy—all I know is that instead of him standing up for Joseph when they were ready to kill him, he said, "Let's sell him instead." Chapter 44 is about God doing a work in the lives of these men to change them, to bring about the wholeness and restoration that needs to happen—and will happen, in chapter 45. Let's take a look:

> Then he commanded the steward of his house, "Fill the men's sacks with food, as much as they can carry, and put each man's money in the mouth of his sack, and put my cup, the silver cup, in the mouth of the sack of the youngest, with his money for the grain." And he did as Joseph told him. (Gen. 44:1–2)

CHANGES

The brothers brought money to buy the grain. Joseph loads up their donkeys with the grain, but then says, "Put the money back in their bags"—the same thing he did last time (which totally panicked them, because they thought they would be accused of stealing the money). Joseph does it again—he's messing with their heads. But then he also takes his silver cup—a sign of Joseph's power, authority and wisdom—and puts it in the bag. Culturally, this was worse than stealing the money!

> As soon as the morning was light, the men were sent away with their donkeys. They had gone only a short distance from the city. Now Joseph said to his steward, "Up, follow after the men, and when you overtake them, say to them, 'Why have you repaid evil for good? Is it not from this that my lord drinks, and by this that he practices divination? You have done evil in doing this.'"
>
> When he overtook them, he spoke to them these words. They said to him, "Why does my lord speak such words as these? Far be it from your servants to do such a thing! Behold, the money that we found in the mouths of our sacks we brought back to you from the land of Canaan. How then could we steal silver or gold from your lord's house? Whichever of your servants is found with it shall die, and we also will be my lord's servants." He said, "Let it be as you say: he who is found with it shall be my servant, and the rest of you shall be innocent." Then each man quickly lowered his sack to the ground, and each man opened his sack. And he searched, beginning with the eldest and ending with the youngest. And the cup was found in Benjamin's sack. Then they tore their clothes, and every man loaded his donkey, and they returned to the city. (Gen. 44:3–13)

See how confident they are of their innocence? "Go ahead and look through our stuff; you're not going to find anything. In fact, if you find it, you can kill whoever has it and make the rest of us your slaves." But notice that the steward changes what the brothers said: "Let it be as you say: he who is found with it shall be my servant, and the rest of you shall be innocent."

The brothers line up, oldest to youngest, so their bags can be searched. Empty, empty, empty, all the way down to the youngest, Benjamin—and they find it! They can't believe it. The Scripture says they tore their clothes because they were so upset. Now, instead of going home with honor and with a ton of food, they are getting hauled back to Joseph as criminals.

How do you think they are feeling now? Scared? Angry? Confused? God wants to change them, to make them grow. But sometimes change hurts, because that's how God gets our attention. Often it is the pain that allows the change to begin.

I loved my first couple of years of marriage. I married my best friend, and it was awesome. But in those first couple of years we fought quite a bit, and it hurt. Why? Because we both had to change. I couldn't stay who I was. And the pain was the impetus that got me to change. I wanted the pain to stop and so I needed to change.

My brother died of cancer at sixteen years of age. God was in the process of reaching me, changing me and growing me into who He wanted me to be. And change hurts. Often pain is exactly what God uses so He can reach our hearts.

C.S. Lewis wrote *A Grief Observed*[1] after his wife died tragically. Lewis said that for him, and he assumed for many, nothing really shakes a man out of his thinking or belief system. He has to literally be knocked silly before he comes to his senses. Lewis actually uses the word torture to describe God's work. He believed that only under torture do we really discover ourselves. Only under that kind of pressure do we truly see the man inside.

Lewis wrote another book called *The Problem of Pain*[2] in which he said that pain "insists" on our attention. Pain wakes you up—in fact, pain will keep you from sleeping altogether. Lewis' most often quoted phrase—"God whispers to us in our pleasures, speaks in our consciences, but shouts in our pain"—comes from his life experience and this book. More than we realize, pain in our lives is the megaphone that God uses to wake us. And these brothers are being awakened from their dead-end lives to be changed into who God created them to be—men who can make an impact for Him.

The same is true for you. God wants to change you, and often, in the early stages, it can hurt, maybe a lot. But don't think that the pain is something to be rushed through. God may want to use it to wake you up so that you can grow and change and make an impact for Him. Maybe today you are in the midst of pain or struggling with hurt. The last thing I want to do is misdiagnose what's happening in your life. But instead of running away from the pain or trying to run through it as fast as you can, maybe you should lean into it. Ask God to show you if there is anything in your heart that needs to change.

That's what's happening here with Judah and his brothers. They had learned to live with deception and lies and it was rotting their lives. On their own, they were not changing. So God introduced a stimulant because he wanted to get their attention. Does God have your attention today?

Change Humbles

> When Judah and his brothers came to Joseph's house, he was still there. They fell before him to the ground. Joseph said to them, "What deed is this that you have done? Do you not know that a man like me can indeed practice divination?" And Judah said, "What shall we say to my lord? What shall we speak? Or how can we clear ourselves? God has found out the guilt of your servants; behold, we are my lord's servants, both we and he also in whose hand the cup has been found." But he said, "Far be it from me that I should do so! Only the man in whose hand the cup was found shall be my servant. But as for you, go up in peace to your father." (Gen. 44:14–17)

When Joseph says, "I'm going to keep Benjamin; you can go back to your father," we know the backstory. We know that Jacob is hyperprotective, and it was all he could do to allow Benjamin to go in the first place. This is a worst case scenario for them. Judah had pledged to be personally responsible for Benjamin. How could he go back without him, knowing the pain it would cause his father? How could he go back and tell his dad that yet another son was gone? And they didn't even take the cup. They were completely innocent!

Judah's response in verse 16, therefore, is very significant: "What shall we say to my lord? What shall we speak? Or how can we clear ourselves? God has found out the guilt of your servants." What guilt? He's not talking about the stolen cup, but about Joseph! It's been twenty years since they sold Joseph, lied to their father and watched him grieve. For twenty years they've hidden the consequences of their choices. It has consumed their entire family.

And now, as God is humbling them before Joseph, the first thing that comes to Judah's mind is "God has found out our guilt." And the weight that is upon them at that moment feels like it is going to crush them as they are told they need to go home and explain to their dad, one more time, that the last remaining son of his beloved Rachel is as dead.

It looks like everything is falling apart—God is finally going to judge them. He's going to come down heavy and hard. They've been trying to outrun Him, but God has finally caught up with them. Have you ever viewed God that way— as if He's pursuing you in anger, waiting for you to slip up so He can finally pay you back for what you've done? That's how Judah felt.

But look—that's not what happens. God doesn't crush them—He's trying to change them into who He longs for them to be. He wants to bring healing, restoration, forgiveness, grace and mercy. But before He can change them, they have to first experience the hurt and be humbled. It's only when they pass through these first two stages that they can get to the third and final step.

Change Requires Coming Clean

> Then Judah went up to him and said, "Oh, my lord, please let your servant speak a word in my lord's ears, and let not your anger burn against your servant, for you are like Pharaoh himself. My lord asked his servants, saying, 'Have you a father, or a brother?' And we said to my lord, 'We have a father, an old man, and a young brother, the child of his old age. His brother is dead, and he alone is left of his mother's children, and his father loves him.'

Then you said to your servants, 'Bring him down to me, that I may set my eyes on him.' We said to my lord, 'The boy cannot leave his father, for if he should leave his father, his father would die.' Then you said to your servants, 'Unless your youngest brother comes down with you, you shall not see my face again.'

When we went back to your servant my father, we told him the words of my lord. And when our father said, 'Go again, buy us a little food,' we said, 'We cannot go down. If our youngest brother goes with us, then we will go down. For we cannot see the man's face unless our youngest brother is with us.' Then your servant my father said to us, 'You know that my wife bore me two sons. One left me and I said, Surely he has been torn to pieces, and I have never seen him since. If you take this one also from me, and harm happens to him, you will bring down my gray hairs in evil to Sheol.'

Now therefore, as soon as I come to your servant my father, and the boy is not with us, then, as his life is bound up in the boy's life, as soon as he sees that the boy is not with us, he will die, and your servants will bring down the gray hairs of your servant our father with sorrow to Sheol. For your servant became a pledge of safety for the boy to my father, saying, 'If I do not bring him back to you, then I shall bear the blame before my father all my life.' Now therefore, please let your servant remain instead of the boy as a servant to my lord, and let the boy go back with his brothers. For how can I go back to my father if the boy is not with me? I fear to see the evil that would find my father." (Gen. 44:18–34)

I've read this section many times, and each time I felt the pain of Judah as he begs for the life of his brother. You have to understand how broken Judah is over what he's put his father through. He's watched the consequences of his choices play out before him, but nobody knows what he's done. He's been living inside this prison of lies, deception and deceit, and it's eating him alive. Now he has to go back to his father, the man that he wounded once when he lied about Joseph, and tell him he's lost Benjamin. As I read this passage, I couldn't help but feel the weight and heaviness and the sadness and the sorrow.

Judah is at a place where God is exerting pressure on him to release what's been inside him, because real change can only happen when we come clean. Do you want to grow? Do you want to make an impact for God? Do you want to change? Then you need to come clean. That's what Judah is wrestling with here. The only way he can resolve this situation is to stop hiding behind this façade he's trying to maintain and come clean, because his life is riddled with sin.

That's something we don't like to talk about too much. We talk about havoc, hurts and dysfunction, but what about sin—those things that put a distance between us and God? Big or small, they chip away at who we are until we are prisoners to the keeping of the lie, desperately trying to keep anyone from finding out who we really are. We live in fear that the lights will come on and people will see us for who we really are. And like Judah and his brothers, we fight to stay in the dark. But because we're in the dark, we never grow. We need to come clean.

During my junior year at Wheaton College, the school installed high-speed internet in all the rooms. (Prior to that, you had to go down to the computer lab.) The school also installed filtering software to block pornographic sites, places you shouldn't go to online. If you tried to go where you shouldn't, a notice popped up on your screen that said "You've been blocked and it's been logged." It must have been written really small, because I don't think anyone noticed what it said.

After a month or two, we got reports of all the sites that students had visited. As an RA (resident assistant), I had to have meetings with students who had been blocked from these sites literally *thousands* of times. We would bring the students in, sit down with them and the conversation would go something like this:

"Do you know why you're here?"

"No, I don't."

"Well, you are here because our records show you tried to access restricted web sites, pornographic web sites."

"No, that's not true. I didn't do that. I wouldn't do that."

Then we would pull out the records of all the web sites they tried to visit, with times and dates. They wouldn't know what to say. We would talk and they would weep.

"I started this when I was younger and I didn't know what to do. I thought when I went to college it would change, I thought it would be different. But it wasn't different and I couldn't change and I've been so afraid that somebody was going to find out what I'm doing."

One kid thought we were going to kick him out. He thought we were going to crush him. But we talked to him about God's forgiveness and about God's mercy. We talked to him about God's love. We talked about restoration in Christ because of who He is and what He's done on the cross. We gave the students strategies: "You need to meet with your RA and enter into an accountability relationship with him. You need to relocate your computer so the screen faces the door."

They loved all those ideas—except for the last suggestion. We told them they had to tell one of their parents and needed to do it that very week. And they needed to have their parents call us so we could talk with them.

That was when the wall would go up. "I can't do that!" they'd say. It was like what Judah must have gone through with his guilt over Joseph. "They'll pull me out of school. They're going to hate me. They can't handle this."

But you've got to come clean. You've got to come out into the light. And for the twenty-some students I met with over that two-week period, the results of talking with their parents were virtually the same: "I have never had such an amazing conversation with my parents before. They forgave me, they love me, they took me in. I feel like a weight has been lifted off my back and I am finally free, I'm finally clean. Now I can grow."

Too often, we think we can practice "sin management." We think we can control it, contain it and keep it over in a corner, and it's not really going to get to us. But sin doesn't work that way. Our relationship with God degenerates into repeatedly asking Him to forgive us for the same stupid thing we asked Him to forgive us for the previous week. We get upset with ourselves and figure that God must be frustrated with us, too, and our relationship starts to crumble. If we want to grow, we've got to come into the light. We've got to come clean.

James 5:16 says, "Therefore, confess your sins to one another and pray for one another, that you may be healed." It's not the job of a priest. It's one man talking to another. It's one woman being real with another. It's a friend asking for prayer. It's a teenage son asking his dad to hold him accountable. It's a daughter being honest with her mom. It's you and your daughter deciding to be vulnerable, to be real, to take things to the next level.

Second Corinthians 5:17 says, "Therefore, if anyone is in Christ, he is a new creation. The old has passed away; behold, the new has come." We can be changed, but we need to come clean. Jesus didn't die on the cross so that we can live mediocre spiritual lives. He came and died and rose so that we could be made new, so that He could remove our sin from us.

Psalm 103:12 says, "As far as the east is from the west, so far does he remove our transgressions from us." God is not out to get you. But God does want to change you. And if you are going to change, it may hurt. You have to be humbled and come clean. But the end result is amazing. You and I have the same opportunity right now. The old can pass, the new can come.

Don't run away from the hurt; don't avoid the humbling. God may be using it to change you. That is the power of the gospel. And living in the reality of that will change us forever. We don't live for ourselves, we live for Christ so that others can experience the same freedom, the same hope, the same change. We live on a mission, as Christ's ambassadors, proclaiming that in Him we can be set free. So how about you?

Remember a few pages back when I asked you to write at the bottom of the page? Well, here's your chance. Take all the time you need and fill in that blank. Write what God's Spirit says to you. You don't need to show it to anybody. Let God's Spirit light up and reveal in your heart something that He wants to change so that He can grow you into who He wants you to be.

Prayer

God, I thank You that You offer us life. Thank You that You offer to change us. I know that sometimes it hurts. I know sometimes it humbles us and we don't like it. And I know that sometimes we get stuck in the dark and we want to stay there. I pray, Jesus, that you would shine Your light on us, that You would illuminate us, that You would reveal what needs to change. God, I pray that You would be with us as we live in the reality of who You are so that we can really be who You made us to be. Thank you that because of Your work on the cross, because You went to the cross willingly, because You allowed Yourself to be killed, we can be made fully alive. God, when we think about all that You have done, we just stand in awe. We are amazed. Thank You for loving us. Thank You that You are not out to get us, but that You want to offer us life, life to the fullest. God, change us. In Jesus' name, Amen.

Chapter 7

TRAVELING LIGHT

Genesis 45

Mike Williams

God wants us to be free.

Do you like to travel? When I was younger, I loved it—and it was so easy. I just stowed whatever I needed into a backpack and took off for a week. Now that I'm married with three little boys, I still like to travel, but it amazes me just how much stuff we have to take with us. On our first family vacation by air, we had a double stroller, our kids' bags, my wife's bag, my bag (all with things stuffed tightly into every available space) and three car seats, since we planned to rent a car. And in my backpack, along with my laptop, we had stuff to keep the boys occupied on the plane: books, games, toys and pillows.

We must have looked like a traveling circus as we headed toward the check-in at the airport, the stroller loaded down with our belongings. Frequent travelers (most of whom had a single carry-on) saw us coming and started picking up their pace to get to check-in before us—they could see the disaster that was about to happen. All the while I kept thinking how much more enjoyable this trip would be if we didn't have all this stuff!

That experience comes flashing back as I think about Joseph and his brothers in Genesis 45. The advantages of traveling light apply to our spiritual journey as well. We may begin our life in Christ with the best of intentions, but as we go along, we start to pick up "stuff"—pain, bad choices and downright sin. Then we start packing all those things down tight into the corners of our souls, hoping we'll never have to deal with them again.

We think we can keep journeying with the Lord, even with all that stuff in there. But after a while, the more stuff we pick up, the more we feel like an overloaded station wagon that's bottoming out every time it goes over a bump—all because we are carrying too much inside our hearts and our souls.

Then one day we get tired of it all. Our walk with the Lord is not going the way it should. Something is just not right; we seem to have lost the joy of the Lord. We can't find it because we are carrying all this stuff around in our hearts and souls that we were never meant to carry.

The good news is Jesus wants us to be free. He doesn't want us lugging around all this stuff in our souls. His burden is easy and light. As we look at this story in Genesis, we can see a very clear path that God uses to walk Joseph's family through this idea and into freedom. It's a path He wants all of us to walk, if we are willing to follow Him.

Joseph has gone on this twenty year roller-coaster ride with his family, and the story has been building toward this climax. He has now risen to power and has a chance to get back at his brothers—if he wants to. Genesis 44 ended with an amazing, emotional appeal from Judah, who offers himself as a slave in place of his younger brother, Benjamin. It's a very tense moment in the story.

Freedom Begins with Recognition

> Then Joseph could not control himself before all those who stood by him. He cried, "Make everyone go out from me." So no one stayed with him when Joseph made himself known to his brothers. And he wept aloud, so that the Egyptians heard it, and the household of Pharaoh heard it. And Joseph said to his brothers, "I am Joseph! Is my father still alive?" But his brothers could not answer him, for they were dismayed at his presence.
>
> So Joseph said to his brothers, "Come near to me, please." And they came near. And he said, "I am your brother, Joseph, whom you sold into Egypt." (Gen. 45:1–4)

Judah has just made an emotional appeal to take Benjamin's place, putting himself at the mercy of Joseph. This is a tense moment, and an eerie kind of quiet settles in that room. What is going to happen next? What is Joseph going to do?

He does something very unexpected. First, he sends the interpreter and all the servants out of the room. The brothers must have thought that was pretty weird because, at that point, they didn't know he could speak their language.

Then he does something even more unexpected—Joseph loses it. He just starts bawling, weeping so loudly that even the people outside the room heard it. He begins to walk toward his brothers, who must have been wondering what was going on.

Finally, he drops the bombshell: "I am Joseph." I'm sure that was the last thing they expected to hear! It says they were "dismayed at his presence." That's rather understated, isn't it? The NIV translation says they were "terrified." I get that. They were shaking in their boots! Joseph is standing before them and you can tell that they don't know what to do.

Joseph realizes this is too much for them to absorb all at once, so he draws them in close and says it again: "Hey, guys, it's me—Joseph—the one you sold into Egypt." His brothers' hearts must have been beating out of their chests. They had to be terrified because standing before them was their worst nightmare—the thing they had been trying to hide for over twenty years. Now it was out in the open and they had to deal with it—all the shame and guilt of the last twenty years came bubbling back to the surface in an instant.

Have you ever been caught in something you were trying to hide? You know the feeling. We think that if we just take our pain, our mistakes, our sins, shove them down into our souls and forget about them, then eventually they will go away. But this story teaches us a very big principle: time does not heal all wounds. Healing comes when you deal with it, when you recognize and acknowledge your sin.

As hard as this was for the brothers, it was exactly where God needed them to be in order to do the work He needed to do in this family. And as hard as it is for us, that's exactly where God needs us to be so He can do His work in our hearts and lives. The only way to get free is to recognize those things we've hidden so deep in our souls and deal with them face-to-face, just like the brothers did.

These hidden things may be our own sins against God and others, or even against ourselves—but not always.

Sometimes we carry around the pain of what others have done to us, things out of our control. We didn't ask for it, but still it happened, causing wounds we carry around in our souls. Sometimes it's the lies we believe about ourselves— lies we've based our life on—and we've shoved them down into our souls and let them weigh us down.

First John 1:7 says, "But if we walk in the light, as he is in the light, we have fellowship with one another, and the blood of Jesus his Son cleanses us from all sin." It can be very difficult and painful, but when we go after that stuff that's been holding us back and bring it into the light, that's where freedom starts.

In the story of Joseph the hidden thing is very obvious—the brothers sold Joseph into slavery—but in our lives, it may not be so easy to recognize. It might be something we considered trivial, but it has affected us much more than we ever even realized.

In my own life, during one of those honest moments before the Lord, I have asked God, "Why does it bother me so much when people don't like me? Why do I sometimes feel like I'm a big disappointment to others?" And God in His grace has shown me that I've been holding on to the pain of a lie that I've believed about myself for a very long time.

In my family, I'm the youngest of four. My three siblings are less than two years apart, and the one closest in age to me is thirteen years older. I grew up thinking that was no big deal, but when people heard about the age gap between my siblings and me, they would usually say, "Oh, I guess you were a surprise, huh?" Or, occasionally, "You were a mistake."

I would kind of laugh it off, but when you hear it often enough, you start to let it sink into your life. I started to think, "Maybe they're right. Maybe I was a mistake. Maybe I wasn't supposed to be here." I started to build on that lie and set out to prove everyone wrong. I was going to do awesome things and show them that I deserve to be here.

I became a people pleaser—someone who needed people's approval more than anything else. I needed to hear, "You did a good job." I hated it, but I couldn't figure out why I was like that until the Lord showed me. He said, "This is why. You have believed a lie in your heart that is not true. You built your life on it and it's changed who you are. It's kept you from walking in the freedom of the person I've made you to be because you live like it's true."

You may have something similar you have packed down deep. Honesty before the Lord about ourselves is one of the first steps in getting free.

When I was little and read the story of Joseph in Sunday school, I looked at him like a superhero—the Teflon Man, because nothing stuck to him. He just kept moving through life and nothing bothered him—God just kept blessing him and doing all these amazing things through him. And that is certainly true. But the more I look at Joseph's life, the more I see that God blessed Joseph because he understood how to honestly deal with his "stuff" before the Lord.

Joseph was a man who felt great emotion. (After all, the guy woke up Pharaoh's household with his crying!) He knew how to let it out, and because of that, God blessed him. He didn't just take his pain and shove it down into his heart and become bitter. He didn't try to deny it and make it on his own. He brought it before the Lord and dealt with it honestly. And because of that, God kept blessing him and using him and helping him walk in that honesty.

Joseph could have taken those twenty years and plotted his revenge. Then when he met his brothers, he could have had his opportunity to carry out that revenge perfectly. But he didn't. He had been walking in freedom before the Lord for the last twenty years and God had blessed that. God can do amazing things through a person like that. God is looking for men and women He can use like Joseph—people He can work through just as powerfully.

We can start the journey toward freedom by doing the hard work of honestly looking at what we've been sticking down in our hearts that we don't want to deal with, and bringing it into the light. It can be painful when God brings these things to light, but He will, because God wants us to be free.

Freedom Flows through Redemption

> And now do not be distressed or angry with yourselves because you sold me here, for God sent me before you to preserve life. For the famine has been in the land these two years, and there are yet five years in which there will be neither plowing nor harvest. And God sent me before you to preserve for you a remnant on earth, and to keep alive for you many survivors. So it was not you who sent me here, but God. He has made me a father to Pharaoh, and lord of all his house and ruler over all the land of Egypt. (Gen. 45:5–8)

After Joseph drops this bombshell on his brothers, they still don't respond! They are probably still running through every possible scenario in their heads: "It's really Joseph! We sold him into slavery and put him through all this pain. What's he going to do to us? Will he throw us in jail? Will he kill us? Will we ever see our families again?"

This powerful ruler of Egypt, second only to Pharaoh, could do whatever he wanted to them. Joseph probably saw that in their eyes and realized he needed to calm them down. He said, "What you did to me wasn't good. I went through years of pain because of it. But God used it to do amazing things. I'm not holding that against you, because what you intended to be bad, God took and used for good."

What Joseph tells them is essentially the Old Testament version of a very familiar New Testament passage, Romans 8:28: "And we know that for those who love God all things work together for good, for those who are called according to his purpose." Both verses point out the key to what it means to walk in freedom: that God can redeem any and every situation in our lives—no matter what it is.

God is in the redemption business, and the most amazing, exciting thing is, He's the only one who can do it! Joseph is taking this opportunity, with his brothers as a captive audience, to teach them about the redemptive power of God. God knew what was going to happen in His sovereignty and, even though the evil actions of Joseph's brothers sent him to Egypt, God took the whole situation and brought good out of it. That's our amazing God!

Imagine your soul as a paper cup. In our journey with the Lord, as we allow these things to get pressed down into our lives—we don't deal with the pain and the choices we've made—and it puts holes in the bottom of the cup, wounds that we're not really ready to deal with. We ask the Lord to fill us, and He is faithful to do what we ask, but the cup doesn't hold water. We are in an endless cycle of asking God to fill us up, but it keeps falling out of us. We haven't let God go deep down into those places in our soul that need to be healed and redeemed so we can walk in freedom.

But when we do, God does what only He can do. He comes in and He heals those areas. He covers them with His blood so that when He fills us up, it doesn't leak out, and we're able to walk in a greater freedom and fullness than ever before. But it only happens when we let Him go to those places and heal them.

The amazing thing about the gospel is not just that Jesus saved us from our sin, which is wonderful. That is only half the story. Though we are saved, sin has left its impact on us—wounds in our hearts—that still needs to be dealt with. The amazing thing about the gospel is not just that Jesus is Savior, but He is also Healer. He can go to those places and heal them.

Isaiah 53:5 says, "But he was pierced for our transgressions; he was crushed for our iniquities; upon him was the chastisement that brought us peace, and with his wounds we are healed." The word for "healed" means more than a physical healing. It means every type of healing that is available to us—physical, emotional, spiritual. All those things were covered in Christ's work on the cross for us.

Freedom Brings Revival

Jesus is able, more than able, to heal all our wounds, if we will let Him. When we do that, freedom starts to flow through us, and the most amazing thing happens. Revival comes out of it.

Starting in verse 9, Joseph is still talking to his brothers. They are still dumbfounded, still wondering what is going to happen, what he plans to do. So Joseph keeps talking to them:

> Hurry and go up to my father and say to him, "Thus says your son Joseph, God has made me lord of all Egypt. Come down to me, do not tarry. You shall dwell in the land of Goshen, and you shall be near me, you and your children and your children's children, and your flocks, your herds, and all that you have. There I will provide for you, for there are yet five years of famine to come, so that you and your household, and all that you have, do not come to poverty." And now your eyes see, and the eyes of my brother Benjamin see, that it is my mouth that speaks to you. You must tell my father of all my honor in Egypt, and of all that you have seen. Hurry and bring my father down here. Then he fell upon his brother Benjamin's neck and wept, and Benjamin wept upon his neck. And he kissed all his brothers and wept upon them. After that his brothers talked with him. (Gen. 45:9–15)

Joseph continues to show amazing grace. Not only does he forgive his brothers, but he asks them to come live with him so he can provide for them. He was so free in his relations with his brothers and what God had done, he was willing to share the best of everything with them. They were just coming here to get food so they wouldn't starve, and now they are going to be living like princes in Egypt.

The last part of this, which is really amazing to me, is that "he fell upon his brother Benjamin's neck and wept, and Benjamin wept upon his neck. And he kissed all his brothers and wept upon them. After that his brothers talked with him." That's the first time in this whole chapter that they have said anything!

How would you like to be a fly on the wall for that conversation? It's been over twenty years. What do you think they talked about? I'm sure they all said they were sorry for what they had done. They probably began asking all the questions that brothers would ask, about family and daily life. It doesn't say how long they talked, but one can imagine it was a long time—they had a lot of catching up to do.

It was only because of Joseph's attitude that they had the freedom to respond to him. All of this was because Joseph was a man who walked in freedom before God, found redemption and revived their relationship. Think of the forgiveness, the reconciliation, the revival of that family, in that room at that moment! It shows what the redemptive power of God can do. But as we read on, we see that not only Joseph and his brothers are revived, but the whole nation of Israel.

In verses 16 to 23, Pharaoh confirms what Joseph has told his brothers. Pharaoh was excited to hear that Joseph's brothers were there, because he loved Joseph. Joseph had done so much for Egypt that Pharaoh wanted the whole family to come. And he gave them provisions for the journey—clothes, money and donkeys laden with gifts for their father.

As they are leaving, Joseph has this last piece of advice for his brothers (which is rather funny when you think about it):

> Then he sent his brothers away, and as they departed, he said to them, "Do not quarrel on the way." (Gen. 45:24)

He still knows his brothers. With eleven brothers, from four different mothers, there is bound to be some tension going on in this family. And he knows them well enough to know they are going to be pointing fingers at each other. ("I told you this was a bad idea; I knew this would happen!") So Joseph says, "Listen, don't ruin this moment with petty arguments. No more fighting. Just hurry home to Dad and tell him what's going on."

But I am sure that on the way back to Canaan, the big question came up: "Who's going to tell Dad?" I mean, who wants to be responsible for that? When they tell their father, they'll have a lot of explaining to do.

> So they went up out of Egypt and came to the land of Canaan to their father Jacob. And they told him, "Joseph is still alive, and he is ruler over all the land of Egypt." And his heart became numb, for he did not believe them. But when they told him all the words of Joseph, which he had said to them, and when he saw the wagons that Joseph had sent to carry him, the spirit of their father Jacob revived. And Israel said, "It is enough; Joseph my son is still alive. I will go and see him before I die." (Gen. 45:25-28)

They not only had to go back and bring the good news, they had to explain to their dad how he came to believe Joseph was dead—that it was their fault. So the freedom that Joseph brought this family also meant that honesty had to happen on the other side. They had to admit that they had lied to their father for twenty years. No wonder his heart went numb.

But as he starts to let it sink in, his heart starts to revive. For the first time in twenty years, his sons are being honest. They are walking in freedom, the freedom that Joseph has displayed to them. They are taking redemption back to their family and because they are willing to do that, their father's heart is revived as well.

That is what freedom leads to: honesty. No more hiding or pretense, no more shoving things down deep into your heart. As you see Jacob come alive, he doesn't want to hear the rest of the story. I can just imagine the brothers trying to explain it all to Jacob, and he says, "That's enough. Joseph is alive and I don't want to waste any more time standing here. Let's go to Egypt. I don't know how much longer I have to live and I want to see my son."

Jacob's family had been revived. And the hope for the Jewish people is revived as well. Jacob moving his family to Egypt is part of the fulfillment of the covenant that God gave Abraham in Genesis 12, where He promised that his descendants would be a great nation. Jacob and his sons became the great Jewish nation because they moved to Egypt, where they were getting the best of everything. And all of that was made possible because Joseph was a man who walked in freedom before the Lord and experienced His redemptive power in his heart and life, and let his family do the same thing. It brought revival to him, his family and the nation of Israel.

Revival is always a personal thing—it starts in us. In my own life, when I let God heal the lies I was building my life on, it brought a level of freedom I had never experienced before. It was a revival. It gave me the ability to love my wife and children in a different way. I was no longer concerned with earning their love, but was free to love them as they were meant to be loved. I didn't try to earn God's approval anymore. I knew that my value was not in anything I did, but in who He said I was and what He did for me on the cross. I'm still a work in progress, but God is doing amazing things.

Revival starts with us, but it overflows to those around us. It may start with you, but it's not just about you. It's about what God wants to do through you. And it starts with these steps for walking in freedom, doing the honest work of going before the Lord and letting Him bring that into your life.

Prayer

Father God, I ask You to speak to me right here and now. I give you permission to go to the places that I have never let You go before, into those places that I have tried to shove so far down in every nook and cranny of my soul and heart, places I never thought anyone could ever find out about. Show me those places. Help me do the work of bringing them into the light. I want to lay it all before You, Lord. I want to leave it all here with You. Show me the path to freedom and help me walk in it for Your glory. In Jesus' name, Amen.

Chapter 8

GOD IS AT WORK

Genesis 46

Marty Berglund

God is at work in your life.

So far, most of the chapters we've been studying have focused on Joseph, but as we look at chapter 46, the story shifts back to Jacob.

It really begins in chapter 37, where Jacob's sons come to him with a bloody tunic to convince him that Joseph is dead, and Jacob goes into grieving for his favorite son. Anyone who has ever lost a child knows the hole in your heart that this leaves. That's why it says that Jacob refused to be comforted.

Can you imagine mourning over the death of your son for twenty years—and then being told he's still alive? Every grieving parent's dream is to wake up and find it was all a mistake, and your child is really alive and well. That's what happens to Jacob. His sons had to come to Jacob and admit that they made up the whole story about the bloody tunic. Can you imagine the confusion, the unbelievable feelings that would rush upon you? And the joy! He can't wait to go see Joseph.

This passage is about moving on in life. Jacob has to literally, physically move—but he also has to move on emotionally and spiritually. We all get stuck at times, and this story is
about how God helps us move on. The key is holding solidly
to a strong conviction that God is at work in your life. This
is what Joseph seems to have, whether he's a slave, whether
he's in prison, no matter what. Now his dad, Jacob, is learning this. I am hoping that as we read through this story, you
and I can learn this too.

God Will Meet with You

> So Israel took his journey with all that he had and came to
> Beersheba, and offered sacrifices to the God of his father
> Isaac. (Gen. 46:1)

Notice that Jacob, at the end of chapter 45, has said, "The
one thing I want to do is see my son before I die." His spirit
was revived and all he wanted to do was see Joseph. We can
understand how anxious he must have been to get to Egypt.
Yet in his anxiousness to get there, he stops to worship the
Lord in a place called Beersheba. He sacrifices to the Lord.

Think about how much time it takes out of his urgent
journey to take a lamb and sacrifice it. He hasn't seen his son
in twenty years, but still he stops and worships the Lord, giving thanks and talking to Him. Why would he do this *now*?
No doubt it helped him get his head straightened out from all
the confusion caused by this remarkable news.

This is what many of us need. Life goes so fast, and we
have so many things we want to accomplish. We are so busy,
with so much to do: taking the kids here, going over there,
fulfilling job responsibilities, spending time on hobbies. We

are so busy with—well, you can fill in the blank. Jacob didn't let that happen. He learned, just as we need to learn, that he needed to make a priority of meeting with God—and look what happened when he did:

> And God spoke to Israel in visions of the night and said, "Jacob, Jacob." And he said, "Here am I." (Gen. 46:2)

When he takes time to meet with God, God speaks to him. Could this be why we don't hear much from God—we don't take the time; we're too busy? I wonder if any of us could have an appointment as urgent as Jacob's. And yet we have no end of excuses for why we can't stop and meet with God. Jacob doesn't make any excuses; he just stops to meet with God, and God speaks to him. Here we learn a very powerful lesson; God will speak to you if you don't get caught up in all the things of life.

This idea that God speaks with people is repeated over and over again in the Bible. God speaks through visions, dreams, prophets, miracles—even, on occasion, in an audible voice. How many times do we have to read it before we believe it? What gets in the way of meeting God? Consider First John 2:15–17:

> Do not love the world or the things in the world. If anyone loves the world, the love of the Father is not in him. For all that is in the world—the desires of the flesh and the desires of the eyes and pride in possessions—is not from the Father but is from the world. And the world is passing away along with its desires, but whoever does the will of God abides forever.

Is this passage saying that all pleasure is wrong, that we shouldn't appreciate beautiful things or that ownership of anything is bad in itself? No. It is saying not to let anything in the world take a priority over God—knowing Him, seeking Him, having a relationship with Him—for the world is passing away.

These desires are wrong only when you let them monopolize and control you, pressuring you out of meeting with God. If you make meeting with God a priority, God can and will speak to you. Right now, do you desperately need to hear from God about your life, your situation, your problem? If you don't hear, it's because you don't have time.

My wife's late uncle was the pastor of a large church on the West Coast. Twenty years ago, as he saw our church growing and was excited about what was going on, he pulled me aside and gave me some wise advice.

"Marty," he said, "you're going awfully fast and doing a lot. You're really busy, and you need to do what I do."

"What's that?" I said.

"You need to take study breaks. You need to get away, to sequester yourself so you can pray and seek God. Do whatever you've got to do to accomplish this, because running the church, and all it involves, it could take you away from God."

So I started putting that discipline in my life, and it helps me stay connected. That doesn't sound like something that only preachers need, does it? Good grief, if I need it, how about you? Have you ever decided to set aside your morning or afternoon to meet with God? Maybe you need to take a whole day, a week or whatever.

I challenge you to do it. You are able to do it—you have access to the Father through Jesus Christ, if you're a Christian. Go to Him—He wants to meet with you. And don't let anything in this world get in your way. Jacob learned that he had to meet with God. Have you learned it? Maybe right now in your own heart you need to make that commitment.

God Will Share His Plan with You

> Then he said, "I am God, the God of your father. Do not be afraid to go down to Egypt, for there I will make you into a great nation. I myself will go down with you to Egypt, and I will also bring you up again, and Joseph's hand shall close your eyes. (Gen. 46:3–7)

You may remember that in Genesis 26, Isaac, Jacob's dad, was living in Canaan, the same place Jacob was living, and there was a famine in the land, just like this one. God specifically came to Isaac and said, "Don't go down to Egypt" (even though Egypt's Nile River made it less susceptible to drought and famine). But now, a generation later, God is telling Jacob to go down to Egypt during the famine.

What we learn from this is that God's plan is different for different people, and different even from generation to generation in the same family. Just because God told His plan to your mom and dad doesn't mean *you* should do what God called *them* to do. You have to seek God for yourself; His plan for you may be totally different.

I once met a guy who was in ministry because his dad was. I don't think that's a good reason to be in ministry. Has God called you? Do you seek God for yourself? That's what Jacob learned. Even though his dad was told not to go down to Egypt, he is to go down. I think that's why God said, "Don't be *afraid* to go down." Jacob may have had "Don't go to Egypt" drummed into him by his father, so God had to say, "I want you to go down; don't be afraid." God's plans are different. His commands, His truth, His morality stay the same; it's not like adultery was sinful then but okay now. Sin is still sin. But His plan and how He carries it out might be different for you.

You may say, "I've walked with the Lord for years and He never seems to show me His plan." Well, if you look at what God says to Jacob, you'll notice that most of it is very general: "Don't be afraid to go down to Egypt . . . I will make you into a great nation . . . I myself will go down with you to Egypt." The only specific thing He says is, "Joseph's hand will close your eyes." So when it comes to knowing God's plan, we have a great advantage over Jacob. We have the experience of generation after generation, general things and specific things, all written down in the Bible! Jacob didn't have that.

God has shared His plan with us if we'll just read it. I am amazed how many Christians are ignorant of the Bible. The words of Almighty God are written down for us to read—and we don't read them, study them, memorize them? What's wrong with us? Why are we so rebellious? The plan is laid out here. Jacob didn't have that, but we do.

Jesus brought this out pretty clearly. Many times as He quoted Scripture, He said, "Have you not read?" Jesus' expectation was that since God recorded the words of all that He's been doing throughout human history in a book, we are supposed to read it. You and I are people of the Book—aren't we supposed to read the Book?

In his book, *A Godward Life*, John Piper, a great thinker and pastor, explains that the church is crippled or made ineffective when we merely read the Word. He says we fall short if our training doesn't include training our minds rigorously to think through the hard or difficult texts. Piper believes that training so we can earn a living is not nearly as important as making sure that the next generation knows and understands the meaning of God's Word. We need to make sure our children and our grandchildren know the meaning of God's Word and that they know how to unlock the riches found there. He warns us not to fail the next generation.[1]

We get so concerned about education. Why aren't we as concerned about education in the most important thing you could possibly learn—the Bible? There are so many other things that we make primary, when they are really secondary to the Bible. I challenge you to read the Word. Read it, study it, memorize it. Train your mind. This is significant if you want to know the plan of God for your life.

God Will Be with You

Verse 4 says, "I myself will go down with you." I don't know how long you've been around, but anyone who has lived long knows that this earth is set in its ways of perversion, sin and depravity, and it's going to be that way until Jesus comes. The best you can have in this life is to have God with you!

That's as good as it's ever going to get. No matter what you have to endure, or what you have to go through, or how joyful life is, or how great things are going, the best you can have is to have the Lord with you. But that really depends on surrendering to Him. He promised in His Word that He'll never leave us or forsake us—the same promise He made to Jacob.

> Then Jacob set out from Beersheba. The sons of Israel
> carried Jacob their father, their little ones, and their wives,
> in the wagons that Pharaoh had sent to carry him. They
> also took their livestock and their goods, which they had
> gained in the land of Canaan, and came into Egypt, Jacob
> and all his offspring with him, his sons, and his sons' sons
> with him, his daughters, and his sons' daughters. All his
> offspring he brought with him into Egypt. (Gen. 46:5-7)

Next it goes on listing name after name after name of all
the people who went with Jacob to Egypt. Look at verse 26
where the story picks up again.

> All the persons belonging to Jacob who came into Egypt,
> who were his own descendants, not including Jacob's
> sons' wives, were sixty-six persons in all. And the sons of
> Joseph, who were born to him in Egypt, were two. All the
> persons of the house of Jacob who came into Egypt were
> seventy. (46:26–27)

What's interesting is that in the Book of Acts it says there
were seventy-five. That's because this was being recounted by
Stephen, who was also counting Ephraim and Ephraim's kids
and grandsons and the same with Manasseh and his grandsons.

> He had sent Judah ahead of him to Joseph to show the
> way before him in Goshen, and they came into the land of
> Goshen. (46:28)

Goshen is outside of Egypt. Joseph had a plan. His family were shepherds. Egyptians don't like shepherds. They
were prejudiced against shepherds. So Joseph figured the
most diplomatic thing was to have them live in Goshen, on
the outskirts of Egypt.

> Then Joseph prepared his chariot and went up to meet
> Israel his father in Goshen. He presented himself to him

and fell on his neck and wept on his neck a good while. Israel said to Joseph, "Now let me die, since I have seen your face and know that you are still alive." Joseph said to his brothers and to his father's household, "I will go up and tell Pharaoh and will say to him, 'My brothers and my father's household, who were in the land of Canaan, have come to me. And the men are shepherds, for they have been keepers of livestock, and they have brought their flocks and their herds and all that they have.' When Pharaoh calls you and says, 'What is your occupation?' you shall say, 'Your servants have been keepers of livestock from our youth even until now, both we and our fathers,' in order that you may dwell in the land of Goshen, for every shepherd is an abomination to the Egyptians." (Gen. 46:29–34)

It says here Joseph presented himself to Jacob and fell on his neck and wept. Have you noticed, in this chapter and the last, there is a lot of weeping going on? In the perfect plan of God for this very righteous man, Joseph, there is weeping!

Somehow we have, in our culture, such an aversion to crying and sorrow and pain that we think no one should ever have to suffer that. Baloney! In the perfect plan of God, in the life of a righteous man like Joseph, there is still weeping—tears of joy and tears of sorrow, all mingled together. There is a place for weeping; it's cathartic. There is even an entire book of the Bible, Lamentations, which is filled with songs of lamenting, complaining to God, weeping.

I've seen people come forward in church and just cry and cry. I know what's going on—they are finally getting honest with God and with themselves, so the tears just flow.

Before I was a Christian, I never cried. I guess you could say I wasn't in touch with my feelings. When I became a

Christian, I was shocked, really shocked, because I started crying about things. I'd be watching a movie and I'd start crying. *What's wrong with me?* I asked myself. I was just getting in touch with my feelings. I'd never done that before, because I was never honest enough.

Then I learned from a professor I had, a Christian psychiatrist, that when you push down your guilt, stuff your anger, fears and anxiety, all the joy and good feelings go down with them. You can't hold one down and not the other.

I never realized that. No wonder I started to have tears of joy and sorrow—emotional healing was taking place in my life like never before. That's what's going on in the passage here. There is emotional healing for Jacob and for Joseph. Maybe that's what you need as well.

People talk about having a good cry, but what's good about it is getting right with the Lord and truthfully sharing your feelings with Him. That was what was happening in the heart of Jacob. He was learning how to really have the Lord with him.

So many Christians I meet have some kind of performance system with God, but it's not really a relationship. A relationship has to be emotional, or it's not real. If we're not real with God, how can we be real with other people, or even with ourselves? Joseph is so real with God, so rich in his relationship with the Lord, it's just beautiful.

Recently, a pastor friend sent me a book by Timothy Keller entitled *Walking with God through Pain and Suffering*, and, not surprisingly, he has a chapter in the book on weeping. What he writes is so profound that I must share it with you.

Keller says that grief and sorrow drive us more into God. He compares this to a thermostat in your home. When it gets colder outside, the thermostat kicks up the furnace. He says that grief and sorrow will drive us into God and show us resources we never knew we had. He tells us to feel the grief. We naturally run from grief and sorrow because we don't want to feel it. We want only the good feelings, the rejoicing.

But Keller points out that Jesus was perfect, and He cried all the time. He was a man of sorrows. Why? Because Jesus *was* perfect—not absorbed with Himself. He could feel the world around Him—the sadness, the hurt and the pain. But Keller says that what you actually have is the joy of the Lord happening inside the sorrow. The weeping drives you into the joy. It doesn't come after the sorrow or the weeping, it happens inside the sorrow and weeping. The weeping drives you into the joy and then the joy enables you to actually feel your grief without it taking you under. He says this makes you emotionally healthy.[2]

That's exactly the way it is. So I'm challenging you right now to cry, weep over your own sin and sickness, stupidity, losses and pain. Weep before the Lord.

If you are not a crying type, that's fine. (I grew up with Scandinavians, and they never cry.) Then just come before the Lord and get honest. That's really what it's all about. Get honest about your feelings—you're mad, you're hurt, whatever. Some of the Psalms are lament songs, where the writer is arguing with God and complaining to God. Go ahead, do that. Learning how to meet with the Lord, how to hear from God and how to have God with us is all about getting honest with the Lord.

The challenges for us from this chapter about Jacob are:

1. Take the time to seek the Lord. He is waiting to meet with you.
2. Read the Book. Study it, memorize it, think about it. God has laid out His plan for you.
3. Cry out to the Lord, weep, talk to Him. Get honest with Him and with yourself.
4. Build a relationship with God. It is the most important thing you will ever do.

Prayer

Lord, I come before you struck by how simple it is to have a relationship with You and horrified at how busy I have made my life. Please give me a burning desire to take the time to know You better. Help me find the time this week to meet with You. Help me spend time in the Book, to see Your plan for my life and answer the questions I have. Father, I pray that You will give me a good dose of honesty. I've been pushing down the guilt, anger, fear and anxiety. I pray that I will get honest with You. If I can weep, hear my sobs. If I cry out to You, hear my prayer. Teach me, oh Lord; I want to learn from You. In Jesus' name, Amen.

Chapter 9

GOD REWARDS THE FAITHFUL

Genesis 47

Marty Berglund

God rewards those who are faithful.

What kind of a person was Joseph? Why we are so attracted to this particular Bible character? Whenever I speak on Joseph, I often hear the comment, "He's my favorite." And yet, he didn't perform any miracles. He didn't preach any great sermons. He didn't write a single paragraph in the whole Bible. So what did he do that was so impressive?

He was faithful—no matter what.

No matter what happened, no matter what twists and turns—betrayal, slavery, prison—the man was faithful. There is, in his incredible example, an attraction that just pulls us in. We long for someone to be faithful. This may be especially true in our culture, where unfaithfulness abounds — in marriages, employment, even church. All this unfaithfulness—where does it come from? Not from the Lord.

What we learn from Joseph is how to be faithful to the Lord. Some of the synonyms found in the thesaurus for the word "faithful" include: *loyal, devoted, steadfast, steady in performance of duty, tried, conscientious, staunch, true, constant, reliable, unwavering, trustworthy, dependable, worthy of confidence, incorruptible, unswerving, resolute, trusting, scrupulous, honest, upright, truthful.* Is it any wonder why people are attracted to Joseph?

Consider the antonyms to "faithful," and it brings Joseph into even sharper focus: *faithless, disloyal, false, traitorous, treacherous, fickle, inconsistent, unstable, unfaithful, untrue, untrustworthy, wavering.*

The power of this man's life was his faithfulness. And although it is God's Spirit that ultimately makes a church great, let's not forget that most churches exist because of faithful people. Faithful involvement—faithful teaching, singing, serving, disciple making—is what builds the church.

In a secular business article I read recently, the author was saying that what really makes a company great is—you guessed it—the *faithfulness* of its employees. And that is also what makes a great church, a great family or a great person. Faithfulness is a powerful dynamic. No church is great because of programs, preaching or leadership—it is *faithful* leaders, *faithful* people, *faithful* servants. And that is exactly what we see in the example of Joseph.

In this unjust, unfair world, where people get taken advantage of and things don't seem to work out like they should, God promises that He will reward faithfulness, whether in this world or in eternity. In light of God's promises to reward faithfulness, there is no reason why you and I should not be faithful.

The question is, how do you do that? What does that look like? In chapter 47 of Genesis, we have a great example of faithfulness. It's the tip of the iceberg; you have to read this in the context of Joseph's whole life to really get it.

Faithful Loyalty

Faithfulness requires loyalty. We see that in the first few verses:

> So Joseph went in and told Pharaoh, "My father and my brothers, with their flocks and herds and all that they possess, have come from the land of Canaan. They are now in the land of Goshen." And from among his brothers he took five men and presented them to Pharaoh. Pharaoh said to his brothers, "What is your occupation?" And they said to Pharaoh, "Your servants are shepherds, as our fathers were." They said to Pharaoh, "We have come to sojourn in the land, for there is no pasture for your servants' flocks, for the famine is severe in the land of Canaan. And now, please let your servants dwell in the land of Goshen." Then Pharaoh said to Joseph, "Your father and your brothers have come to you. The land of Egypt is before you. Settle your father and your brothers in the best of the land. Let them settle in the land of Goshen, and if you know any able men among them, put them in charge of my livestock." (Gen. 47:1–6)

Do you notice here, over and over again Joseph shows his loyalty to his dad, to his brothers (in spite of them selling him into slavery), to his boss, Pharaoh, and most of all, to God?

A seminary professor of mine had done some study on the land of Goshen and had even traveled there. He just loved to talk about what an incredible place it was—the best land for crops, as well as being strategically located for the trade routes that went through the area. This is why the Israelites prospered so much there. But the other reason Joseph requested Goshen was because he knew Egyptians didn't like shepherds, and Goshen was outside of town. Joseph had it all worked out. His loyalty even extended to his employer's sensibilities.

Joseph saved the lives of his entire family by putting this wise plan together. He was loyal to his father and his brothers in spite of what they had done, and loyal to his boss. How did he get to be this way?

In the book of Proverbs we get a hint. Proverbs 1:7 says, "The fear of the Lord is the beginning of knowledge; fools despise wisdom and instruction." Joseph had "the fear of the Lord"—respect, honor, reverence for the Lord—and that, of course, includes loyalty. How did Joseph become this kind of a person? The answer is clear: he had loyalty to the Lord. He hung onto the Lord no matter what—whether betrayed by his brothers, sold into slavery or thrown into prison. He became a leader because of his loyalty to the Lord through the whole thing.

In his book on the life of Joseph, Max Lucado tells a story about a young boy who is now a high school football player. He remembers when the boy was seven years old and was diagnosed with cancer. They had to do surgery and chemotherapy—several months of very strenuous prayers and treatments. It gives him great joy to watch him play football in high school. But the most interesting thing about the story is how this little seven-year-old was diagnosed with cancer.

Max says this kid was horsing around with his cousins and got kicked in the gut. He went crying to his mom, telling her about how much it hurt. Days later, his stomach still hurt, so his mom took him to the doctor. The wise doctor decided to run some tests and sent him to a specialist. After more testing they found a little tumor behind his spleen, did surgery to remove it and discovered it was cancerous. Then the chemotherapy began.

The boy's father asked the surgeon if he could estimate how long the tumor had been there. The doctor said that, based on the type and size of the tumor, it could only have been there a short time, perhaps even just a few days.

A few days? The tumor was identified that early only because they did so many tests. So this kid is now playing football, healthy and strong, because of a kick in the gut?

Lucado went on to tell another story about a three-year-old girl named Isabel who had never lived anywhere but in a Nicaraguan orphanage. Her chance of being adopted was slim, because parents usually want children under two. One day Isabel was running outside to play when the door slammed on her finger. This poor little girl, with no mom, no dad, no hope for a future, has to have her finger slammed in the door? It just didn't seem fair.

But the story continues. When her finger was slammed in the door, there happened to be an American visiting the orphanage, Ryan Schnoke. He was there trying to adopt a child, but it wasn't working out. No other adults were around at the time, so when Ryan heard the little girl screaming in pain, he ran out to the playground, picked her up and comforted her.

Several months later, as Ryan and his wife were about to give up any hope of adopting, Ryan remembered Isabel and decided to try once more, and this time the adoption went through. Now this girl is being raised in America all because she got her finger slammed in the door.[1]

Isn't it amazing how God does things? God uses a guy sold into slavery by his brothers and thrown into prison. God uses a kick in the gut or a finger slammed in a door.

A friend of mine is the pastor of a new church in Tuckerton, New Jersey. God called the church to buy an old car dealership and remodel it into a church building. They started to fix it up but they couldn't get an occupancy permit without spending more money—money they didn't have. The whole deal was falling apart, and they prayed, "Lord, why did You have us buy this place? It's killing us. We can't afford it. It's not working. And now, we can't even use it."

Then Hurricane Sandy hit and Tuckerton needed help. The township came to the church and said, "We have to use your building as a shelter."

My friend said, "Sorry, but we don't have an occupancy permit."

And the township said, "Well, you do now!" Since then, the church has just exploded. And they have been a major source of help in Tuckerton.

Isn't it amazing the way God does things? But you have to stay faithful, loyal to the Lord in the midst of the kick in the gut, and the finger slammed in the door and no occupancy permit.

I thank God that there are people in my church who have been faithful, trusting God through good times and bad, for twenty or thirty years. It is those faithful people, who will be loyal no matter what, that really build the kingdom. This is what our country and our churches need so badly. With unfaithful pastors and parishioners, people not loyal to the Lord anymore, we're falling apart. We need Josephs.

Faithful Endurance

> Then Joseph brought in Jacob his father and stood him before Pharaoh, and Jacob blessed Pharaoh. And Pharaoh said to Jacob, "How many are the days of the years of your life?" And Jacob said to Pharaoh, "The days of the years of my sojourning are 130 years. Few and evil have been the days of the years of my life, and they have not attained to the days of the years of the life of my fathers in their days of their sojourning." And Jacob blessed Pharaoh and went out from the presence of Pharaoh. Then Joseph settled his father and his brothers and gave them a possession in the land of Egypt, in the best of the land, in the land of Rameses, as Pharaoh had commanded. And Joseph provided his father, his brothers, and all his father's household with food, according to the number of their dependents. (Gen. 47:7–12)

Notice that Jacob says, "My years have been few and evil." That's how he talks about his life. Now contrast that with what Joseph said about his life in chapter 45 when he tells his brothers who he is.

> So Joseph said to his brothers, "Come near to me, please." And they came near. And he said, "I am your brother, Joseph, whom you sold into Egypt. And now do not be distressed or angry with yourselves because you sold me here, for God sent me before you to preserve life. For the famine has been in the land these two years, and there are yet five years in which there will be neither plowing nor harvest. And God sent me before you to preserve for you a remnant on earth, and to keep alive for you many survivors. So it was not you who sent me here, but God. He has made

me a father to Pharaoh, and lord of all his house and ruler over all the land of Egypt." (Gen. 45:4-8)

He tells his brothers, "Don't beat yourselves up about what you did. God orchestrated all this. When you sold me into slavery, God was there. When I was in prison, God was there. And after I got out of prison, God was there." He sees God before, God in the middle and God at the end. Talk about endurance! That's how he could endure all that—he saw God. This is the key to his whole life.

It should be the key to our life, too. We should see God in the midst of it. But do we just see our problems—childlessness, divorce, cancer? If we don't see God before, during and after the childlessness, the divorce, the cancer, then this is the key we need to pick up on. It's the only way you can endure—you've got to see the Lord.

This contrast between Joseph and his dad really speaks volumes, doesn't it? "Few and evil are the days of my life"? Where is the Lord in this? Jacob can't see Him. But his son, Joseph, sure does.

Focus on the Lord—that's really the only way you can endure anything. That's what we learn from Joseph.

Faithful Dependability

As the famine gets more severe, Egypt becomes the wealthiest nation in the entire world at that time. The situation gets very interesting:

Now there was no food in all the land, for the famine was very severe, so that the land of Egypt and the land of Canaan languished by reason of the famine. And Joseph gathered up all the money that was found in the land of

Egypt and in the land of Canaan, in exchange for the grain that they bought. And Joseph brought the money into Pharaoh's house. And when the money was all spent in the land of Egypt and in the land of Canaan, all the Egyptians came to Joseph and said, "Give us food. Why should we die before your eyes? For our money is gone." And Joseph answered, "Give your livestock, and I will give you food in exchange for your livestock, if your money is gone." So they brought their livestock to Joseph, and Joseph gave them food in exchange for the horses, the flocks, the herds, and the donkeys. He supplied them with food in exchange for all their livestock that year. And when that year was ended, they came to him the following year and said to him, "We will not hide from my lord that our money is all spent. The herds of livestock are my lord's. There is nothing left in the sight of my lord but our bodies and our land. Why should we die before your eyes, both we and our land? Buy us and our land for food, and we with our land will be servants to Pharaoh. And give us seed that we may live and not die, and that the land may not be desolate."

So Joseph bought all the land of Egypt for Pharaoh, for all the Egyptians sold their fields, because the famine was severe on them. The land became Pharaoh's. As for the people, he made servants of them from one end of Egypt to the other. Only the land of the priests he did not buy, for the priests had a fixed allowance from Pharaoh and lived on the allowance that Pharaoh gave them; therefore they did not sell their land.

Then Joseph said to the people, "Behold, I have this day bought you and your land for Pharaoh. Now here is seed for you, and you shall sow the land. And at the harvests you shall give a fifth to Pharaoh, and four fifths shall be your own, as seed for the field and as food for yourselves and your households, and as food for your little ones." And they said, "You have saved our lives; may it please my lord, we will be servants to Pharaoh." So Joseph made it a statute concerning the land of Egypt, and it stands to this day, that Pharaoh should have the fifth; the land of the priests alone did not become Pharaoh's.

Thus Israel settled in the land of Egypt, in the land of Goshen. And they gained possessions in it, and were fruitful and multiplied greatly. And Jacob lived in the land of Egypt seventeen years. So the days of Jacob, the years of his life, were 147 years.

And when the time drew near that Israel must die, he called his son Joseph and said to him, "If now I have found favor in your sight, put your hand under my thigh and promise to deal kindly and truly with me. Do not bury me in Egypt, but let me lie with my fathers. Carry me out of Egypt and bury me in their burying place." He answered, "I will do as you have said." And he said, "Swear to me"; and he swore to him. Then Israel bowed himself upon the head of his bed. (Gen. 47:13–31)

There seems to be no hint in this passage at all that the people feel abused or taken advantage of by Joseph. They literally said to him, "You have saved our lives by letting us be your servants." So it wasn't the kind of slavery that we often think of. As for Israel, in verse 27 it says, "They gained possessions in the land and they became fruitful and they multiplied greatly."

How did Joseph do all this? He was dependable. His faithfulness, reflected through his dependability, became something all the people recognized. They knew they could trust Joseph; after all, he had saved their lives. Could he have taken advantage of them? Of course, he could have. A dictator would have done such a thing, but not Joseph.

When they ran out of money, livestock and land, Joseph gave them grain to plant (on land that was now owned by the Pharaoh) and made a deal with them to pay Pharaoh back with just a fifth of the harvest. (They kept four-fifths, which was a pretty good deal, since they didn't own the seed or the land. They were just sharecroppers.) Joseph could have demanded half or three-fourths of the harvest, but he made a generous offer to them and they took it. Why? Because Joseph was dependable; they could trust him to deal fairly with them. Faithful people are dependable people.

I want to share a statement written by the late Christian author Tim Hansel about his mother. He called it "Great Lady":

> I remember when I was in fourth grade and you used to do things like stay up half the night just to make me a Zorro outfit for Halloween. I knew you were a good mom, but I didn't realize what a great lady you were.
>
> I can remember you working two jobs sometimes and running the beauty shop in the front of our home so as to insure [sic] that our family would be able to make ends meet. You worked long, long hours and somehow managed to smile all the way through it. I knew you were a hard worker, but I didn't realize what a great lady you were. . . .
>
> I can remember junior high and high school, you helping me muddle through my homework—you making costumes for special events at school—you attending all my games. I knew at the time that you would try almost anything if it would help one of your children, but I didn't realize what a great lady you were.

I remember bringing forty-three kids home at 3:30 one morning when I worked for Young Life and asking if it would be okay if they stayed over for the night and had breakfast. I remember you getting up at 4:30 a.m. to pull off this heroic feat. I knew at the time that you were a joyous and generous giver, but I didn't realize what a great lady you were. . . .

I remember all the sacrifices you made so that I could go to Stanford, the extra work you took on, the care packages you sent so regularly, the mail that reminded me that I wasn't doing this all alone. I knew you were a great friend, but I didn't realize what a great lady you were.

I remember graduating from Stanford and deciding to work for two hundred dollars a month loving kids through Young Life. Although you and Dad thought I had fallen off the end of the ladder, you still encouraged me. In fact, I remember when you came down to help me fix up my little one room abode. You added your special, loving touch to what had been very simple quarters. I realized then—and time and time again—what a creative genius you were, but I didn't realize what a great lady you were.

Time wore on, I grew older and got married and started a family. You became "Nana" and cherished your new role, yet you never seemed to grow older. I realized then that God had carved out a special place in life when He made you. But I didn't realize what a great, great lady you were.

I got slowed down by an accident, things got a little tougher for me but you stood alongside me as you always had.

Some things, I thought, never change—and I was deeply grateful. I realized then what I had known for a long time, what a great nurse you can be—but I didn't realize what a great, great lady you were. . . .

> In the last year, when you have had to stand alone as never before [his father had died], all of what I had observed and experienced all those years has come together in a brand new way. In spite of it all, now your laughter is richer, your strength is stronger, your love is deeper and I am discovering in truth what a great, great lady you are.[2]

What a testament to dependability! In contrast to that, I recently talked to three men in their 20s, all coming out of families in divorce—the dad not faithful, the mom not faithful, no dependability. And all three of these young Christians said to me, "I want to be the dad I never had. I want to create a family that can avoid the sorrow over no dependability, over faithlessnes." That's what is tearing this country apart, tearing companies apart, tearing churches apart, tearing families apart and tearing lives apart. What you need to be as a Christian is faithful.

Maybe you'll never perform a miracle, and you'll never write a chapter in the Bible or be famous for anything—so what? That's not what makes a country great, a family great, a person great. Faithfulness does. And Scripture has spelled it out for you: it's being loyal; it's focusing on the Lord so you can endure; it's being a dependable person.

No one but the Lord in your life can pull that off. That's the only way we can stay faithful, because we all have a tendency not to be. Only God can make you faithful.

Prayer

Lord, I see the life of Joseph and I am so impressed. So few can measure up to Joseph; I know I can't. But Lord, I want to be faithful—faithful to my spouse, my children, my church, my community. I want to be a faithful person, one that is dependable, one that is loyal, one that can endure hardship no matter what, because I focus like a laser on the Lord. Lord, I'm here to learn how to be faithful and I'm making a decision right now—I will be faithful to You for the rest of my days. Give me the strength, give me the power, because I don't have it, to be faithful. In Jesus' name, Amen.

Chapter 10

FINISHING STRONG

Genesis 48

Marty Berglund

The key to finishing strong.

In Genesis 48 Jacob is near the end of his life and is trying to pass on some things to his children. This is highly instructive for us on how to finish well, how to finish strong. Jacob, who wasn't always strong, is now going to finish strong.

When Dr. Gene Getz spoke at our church, he shocked many of us when he told us he was eighty-one years old. He's traveling around the world teaching the Bible, he has written about sixteen books and he had just finished editing and writing a new Bible with QR codes that take you to over 120 hours of video.[1] It's pretty impressive that he has that much stamina—and it's not just physical stamina; it's spiritual stamina. He is very strong in his faith and clear about his hope for the future—not just about going to heaven, but about what he can do while he is still here on earth. He has a deep, profound love for people.

He didn't even get a chance to tell us about some of the trials, tribulations and difficulties he's been through. It's an amazing story. But how is he finishing so strong? Not everyone does, not even everyone in ministry. Sometimes even admirable Bible characters finished rather poorly, giving up on things, like Solomon.

It makes you wonder—how has Dr. Getz been able to finish so strong? That's what I want to do. Whether my finish line is sooner or later, I want to finish strong. I want to be able to leave a legacy, to make a difference. Don't you?

This passage teaches us how to do that. At the end of Jacob's life, he is finishing very strong, and he gives us clues as to how we can finish strong as well.

Jacob was not always spiritually strong. He started out by cheating his brother out of his birthright, and his brother hated him. They eventually resolved all that, but remember also that he deceived his father—wearing that goat skin to pretend he was Esau so his dad would give the blessing to him. Lying, manipulating, deceiving—that's how Jacob starts out.

But look how he ends up. If you read carefully through the book of Genesis, chapter after chapter, you'll see how he changes. And he has a son named Joseph who is just stellar in his trust of God. Joseph's faith seems to even stimulate Jacob as he watches his son believe God. So he finishes well even though he started out weak.

Maybe you can relate. Maybe you messed up for a while too, like Jacob. Maybe you didn't start out so well, and you've done some things you regret. So did Jacob, but he finished strong, and he gives all of us hope that no matter what we've done, no matter how we've messed up, we can finish strong, too. Let's look for the clues.

Don't Forget What God Has Done in Your Past

> After this, Joseph was told, "Behold, your father is ill." So
> he took with him his two sons, Manasseh and Ephraim.
> And it was told to Jacob, "Your son Joseph has come to
> you." Then Israel summoned his strength and sat up in
> bed. And Jacob said to Joseph, "God Almighty appeared
> to me at Luz in the land of Canaan and blessed me, and
> said to me, 'Behold, I will make you fruitful and multiply
> you, and I will make of you a company of peoples and will
> give this land to your offspring after you for an everlast-
> ing possession.' And now your two sons, who were born
> to you in the land of Egypt before I came to you in Egypt,
> are mine; Ephraim and Manasseh shall be mine, as Reu-
> ben and Simeon are. And the children that you fathered
> after them shall be yours. They shall be called by the name
> of their brothers in their inheritance. As for me, when I
> came from Paddan, to my sorrow Rachel died in the land
> of Canaan on the way, when there was still some distance
> to go to Ephrath, and I buried her there on the way to
> Ephrath (that is, Bethlehem)." (Gen. 48:1–7)

When Jacob says, "God Almighty appeared to me at Luz,"
he is referring back to the story in Genesis 28, when he saw
a vision of a ladder to heaven and angels are ascending and
descending. God was saying to Jacob, "You think you are in
control of your fate. That's why you manipulate and connive
to get your way. But I've got it all in control. My angels are
going back and forth. I'm in charge." The Bible doesn't tell
us, but I imagine the entire story, detail by detail, was told to
Joseph and his sons.

This is not just an old man reminiscing. This is a very
significant thing Jacob is doing. If you notice in verse 2, it
says he "summoned his strength," which means this weak,

dying man struggled to sit up in bed because he was going to say something very important.

He goes on to tell what God revealed to him: "Behold, I will make you fruitful and multiply you, and I will make of you a company of peoples and will give this land to your offspring after you for an everlasting possession." Jacob is basically telling what God has done in his life—how God met with him and spoke to him. He wants his sons to understand this profound event and the promise God gave to him—similar to the one God had given to his father, Isaac, and his grandfather, Abraham.

Part of Jacob finishing strong was passing on to the next generation what he had learned about God, what he had observed. Many Christian men and women don't tell their kids or their grandkids the story of God in their life. Do you ever take the opportunity, like Jacob is doing here, to tell your children and grandchildren the story of how you became a Christian? Do they know the story of how God met you in a significant way and helped you find your spouse or got you through certain trials or tribulations—the victories God has given you in life?

We have this idea that education or teaching is best left to some qualified teacher, other than ourselves. When do you tell your story to your kids? When do you tell them about your victories or the spiritual lessons you have learned? It is so significant to be able to pass that on to your children.

Jacob is also alluding to something significant in verse 5 when he says, "Ephraim and Manasseh shall be mine, as Reuben and Simeon are." Jacob is saying that as he hands out his inheritance to his twelve sons, Ephraim and Manasseh are to be considered like his own children. He has a conviction that this was what God wanted, so he is making it very clear.

Do your kids, your grandkids, your friends, your relatives, know *your* convictions? Our kids, our relatives, our friends, need to understand that in life, we've learned a few things and we have some strong convictions about things. You finish strong when you take the opportunity to speak into the lives of your kids, your grandkids or others younger than you.

I mentioned Dr. Gene Getz earlier. Can you imagine what it did to me when I was twenty-six or twenty-seven years old and that man, who was in his late forties at that time, actually treated me like I had something going—like I could be somebody? He would take me aside and speak into my life. He helped me get ordained in the ministry. It meant so much that someone older actually believed in me.

I conducted a funeral once in which I was surprised that so little was said during the service about the deceased man and his faith in Christ. So in my eulogy, I shared a few things that this man had told me in the last part of his life about his relationship with God—some of his convictions, some of what God had taught him. I didn't think it was very earth-shattering or anything. But when we got to the graveside with just the family, his son and daughter came up to me and said, "We didn't know our dad thought and said those things."

That made me unbelievably sad. If only their dad had told them how he felt about them, about life, about God, it could have changed everything. This guy totally blew it! I'm glad he told me, his pastor, but he should have told his kids. It would have changed his relationship with them, as well as their relationship with the Lord.

I'm not talking about lecturing your children or badgering them, I'm just talking about sharing. It's an important thing to do. I read this question recently: *After your kids have spent all their inheritance, what will they have left?* Something to think about, isn't it?

Remember to Bless Those Who Carry On after You

When Israel saw Joseph's sons, he said, "Who are these?" Joseph said to his father, "They are my sons, whom God has given me here." And he said, "Bring them to me, please, that I may bless them." Now the eyes of Israel were dim with age, so that he could not see. So Joseph brought them near him, and he kissed them and embraced them. And Israel said to Joseph, "I never expected to see your face; and behold, God has let me see your offspring also." Then Joseph removed them from his knees, and he bowed himself with his face to the earth. And Joseph took them both, Ephraim in his right hand toward Israel's left hand, and Manasseh in his left hand toward Israel's right hand, and brought them near him. And Israel stretched out his right hand and laid it on the head of Ephraim, who was the younger, and his left hand on the head of Manasseh, crossing his hands (for Manasseh was the firstborn). And he blessed Joseph and said, "The God before whom my fathers Abraham and Isaac walked, the God who has been my shepherd all my life long to this day, the angel who has redeemed me from all evil, bless the boys; and in them let my name be carried on, and the name of my fathers Abraham and Isaac, and let them grow into a multitude in the midst of the earth."

When Joseph saw that his father laid his right hand on the head of Ephraim, it displeased him, and he took his father's hand to move it from Ephraim's head to Manasseh's

head. And Joseph said to his father, "Not this way, my father; since this one is the firstborn, put your right hand on
his head." But his father refused and said, "I know, my son,
I know. He also shall become a people, and he also shall be
great. Nevertheless, his younger brother shall be greater
than he, and his offspring shall become a multitude of nations." So he blessed them that day, saying, "By you Israel will pronounce blessings, saying, 'God make you as
Ephraim and as Manasseh.'" Thus he put Ephraim before
Manasseh. (Gen. 48:8–20)

See what is going on here? Jacob is crossing his hands,
putting his right hand on Ephraim, the younger son, instead
of Manasseh, the firstborn. Ephraim was getting the blessing normally reserved for the firstborn (remember how Jacob, the younger son, stole Esau's firstborn blessing?). It actually came true—Ephraim became one of the major leaders
of Israel.

It's also a double blessing for Joseph. There are twelve
tribes in Israel, so Joseph gets a blessing. But he gets two
blessings. Jacob is elevating Joseph's two sons Manasseh and
Ephraim up to the level of being like his own sons.

Let's dig a little deeper on this. Look at First Chronicles
5:1–2:

The sons of Reuben the firstborn of Israel (for he was
the firstborn, but because he defiled his father's couch, his
birthright was given to the sons of Joseph the son of Israel, so that he could not be enrolled as the oldest son; though
Judah became strong among his brothers and a chief came
from him, yet the birthright belonged to Joseph).

Did you see that? The firstborn son, Reuben, is removed
from his position because of his immorality. We will see that
in the next chapter; morality does make a difference in your

life. But, now Ephraim and Manasseh become the head, especially Ephraim.

There are two things I wanted to mention here. The first is: when you speak into your children's lives, tell them what they could be. This is what Jacob is doing here. If you are a parent, are you taking the opportunity to bless your children?

At a Promise Keepers' event I was attending, a preacher from Atlanta challenged the men to do what he called prophesying over your children. That's just a different way of saying the same thing. Put your blessing on your kids, he said, by telling them what they could be. Tell them the great gifts, talents and abilities you see in them.

That's kind of what Dr. Getz did for me. He spoke into my life. Speak into your kids' lives or the life of someone younger than you, someone that isn't as far along. I do this now with younger pastors. I tell them, "I see great potential in you. Look what God's already done in your life. It looks like He's leading you in this or that direction."

The second thing you need to tell your kids is how they must trust God. Very often people think that it's just your talent, ability and strength that carry you along, but it's not. Yes, you need some talent and some strength, but it's got to be the Lord because you're not going to make it any other way. Maybe it's because I'm older now, but it's easier for me to admit that I can't make it without the Lord. No matter how gifted and talented you are, it is the Lord who sustains you.

Remind Everyone of God's Faithfulness

> Then Israel said to Joseph, "Behold, I am about to die, but God will be with you and will bring you again to the land of your fathers." (Gen. 48:21)

This verse just jumps off the page with the words, "God *will . . .*" Jacob is very clearly expressing his confidence in God to provide for his descendants.

I mentioned earlier that Dr. Getz was a mentor to me and is still going strong. Another friend of mine, who was the same age as Dr. Getz, was also a mentor to me, but he didn't finish very strong. In contrast to trusting God as Dr. Getz does, he became a cynical, doubting, grumpy old man. Yes, even preachers can become grumpy old men. This other man also had a big church, great influence and great speaking ability. But he didn't stay focused. He started to hold grudges and take things personally that he should have trusted to the Lord.

It is easy to say we trust the Lord, to start well and even to be effective and highly gifted, but if you don't keep looking to the Lord and believe that "God will," like Jacob, you will fall short. Jacob came to the conclusion, even in his old age, that "God will" provide and "God will" take care of you.

My friend Dr. Getz has had his share of disappointments and difficult times. He would say you haven't heard half the stories of things that he had to go through. But he keeps believing that "God will," that God is faithful. He is finishing very strong. My other friend and former mentor did not finish so strong, even to the point that he told me at times, "Don't do what I did." Follow God, trust Him, He is faithful.

I can't finish strong for you, and no one else can. You have to make the decision, even right now, to believe that "God will" and put your faith and trust in Him. Remind yourself of God's faithfulness to you in the past and pass on to others what God has done. It seems as if the older you get, the more opportunities you have.

Prayer

Lord, as I look back at my life, I, like Jacob, have decisions to make. I remember my failures, the things I haven't done, the things I have done, and I forget all that You have done. Thank you, Lord, for what you have done in my past. Show me who I can share my story with—a friend, a relative, a child, a grandchild. Whom can I tell how faithful You are? Lord, give me a chance to speak into someone's life, show me who I can bless on my way out as I'm getting older. Remind me daily that God is faithful and that "God will"—God will save me, God will honor His word. In Jesus' name, Amen.

Chapter 11

GOD IS GOOD

Genesis 49 & 50

Marty Berglund

What God means for you is good!

Living the Christian life is a process. It's not a one-and-done thing. After you take the first step, you need to take another step and another after that. God designed it that way—a step-by-step process to grow and develop as a Christian.

Some of those steps may be easy, like going downhill; some may be hard, like going uphill. Some steps may be fast, like running, while others may be very slow, a real struggle. But one thing is perfectly clear: unless you take steps, you won't grow.

Many people are stunted in their Christian life because they've stopped taking steps. I have close friends who used to be really stepping, but then they stopped. Some of them were pastors, but they got so stunted they quit the ministry. Some of them didn't even notice they had stopped taking steps, because they were just coasting.

If you see yourself in that description, the last two chapters of Genesis are just what you need to shake you up, to show you the next step you need to take in your walk with God. And these chapters center on one simple concept: God is good and what He means for you is good.

God does not mean to destroy you, to harm you or to cheat you out of your life. But this is precisely where we often struggle in our walk with God. We hesitate to take the next step, and get stunted, or even go backwards, because we struggle with the idea that God is good and the next step He has for us is good, even though it may be a hard, uphill struggle.

This is precisely why we admire Joseph. Sold into slavery by his brothers—he keeps stepping. Put in jail—he keeps stepping. Next thing you know, he is head of all Egypt. Why? Because he kept stepping, even when the stepping was hard, when it was difficult to trust God.

Not only Joseph, but as we saw in the last chapter, his dad, Jacob, is taking steps as well. Jacob was stunted for a while. But he ended up finishing quite well because he started taking steps again. Maybe you haven't taken steps for a while in your walk with God. Here is your opportunity. Let's look at the steps you may need to take in your walk with God.

God's Morality Is Good for You

Let's set the context before we look at the passage. In chapter 49 Jacob calls in all twelve of his boys and says to them, "I'm about to die. Here are my final words to you." It's kind of a blessing, but also kind of a prophecy. It is based on the idea of what we call moral code. The Bible teaches very clearly that when God created humanity He put a moral code in our hearts. Look at Romans 2:14–16:

> For when Gentiles, who do not have the law, by nature do what the law requires, they are a law to themselves, even though they do not have the law. They show that the work of the law is written on their hearts, while their conscience also bears witness and their conflicting thoughts accuse or even excuse them on that day when, according to my gospel, God judges the secrets of men by Christ Jesus.

Paul is describing the human conscience—the innate ability to see that some things are right and some are wrong, some things are good and some are bad. Where did this come from? *Mere Christianity*, by C.S. Lewis, a book I highly recommend, is based on that idea. Lewis, an atheist who became a Christian, said that somehow in humanity, we know some things are just wrong; they are bad. How do we know that? Because there is a God and He put this moral code, described in Romans as a law, written on our hearts, and we sense it.[1]

On the basis of that moral code, Jacob blesses his boys and tells about their future, depending on how they responded to the moral code.

> Then Jacob called his sons and said, "Gather yourselves together, that I may tell you what shall happen to you in days to come." (Gen. 49:1)

> These sons are the twelve tribes of Israel. This is what their father said to them as he blessed them, blessing each with the blessing suitable to him. (49:28)

Let's sum up these blessings of Jacob:
1. Reuben—"Fornication can ruin your future."
2. Simeon and Levi—"Revenge doesn't pay off." (If you remember, in Genesis 34, they instigated an attack on Shechem and his city in revenge for the rape of

their sister and killed many innocent people. Some
of the things Jacob says aren't so blessing-like!)

3. Judah—"Holding to your morals brings honor." (Judah was upright and did have moral values.)
4. Zebulun—"Strong morals bring rest to your soul."
5. Issachar—"Laziness leads to being used."
6. Dan—"Idolatry will cost you dearly." (He was an idolater.)
7. Gad—"Nothing beats perseverance."
8. Asher—"Use the gifts wisely that God gives you."
9. Naphtali—"Good words will set you free."
10. Joseph—"Those who suffer for righteous morals will be rewarded."
11. Benjamin—"Cruelty will ruin your life."

As you read through Jacob's words, the teaching is very
clear: accept God's moral code and you will find blessing; reject it and you will find trouble. If the moral code is written
on our hearts and we follow it, we are going to be blessed.
Jacob is encouraging those who need encouragement and
warning those who need warning. He is hoping, I think, that
some of them will change.

This is an encouragement and a warning for our day
and age. From the way some people in our culture talk, the
jokes they tell and the way they act, you would think morals didn't really matter. That's just plain wrong; morals do
make a difference.

Here in the very first book of the Bible, the principle
that God will judge according to His moral code written on
the hearts of human beings is established. Morals do matter,
Jacob would say. It makes a big difference how you act, how

you joke, what you think about, how you treat others. This reminds me of Second Thessalonians 2:3–4:

> Let no one deceive you in any way. For that day will not come, unless the rebellion comes first, and the man of lawlessness is revealed, the son of destruction, who opposes and exalts himself against every so-called god or object of worship, so that he takes his seat in the temple of God, proclaiming himself to be God.

Notice what the Antichrist is called: the man of lawlessness! He's described as a man who does not follow God's moral code, who is lawless. Those who are lawless become a law unto themselves—they only do what they want to do; they make their own rules. What does that lead to? He is revealed as the son of destruction. When you reject God's moral code for your life and you make up the rules as you go along, according to what you want to do or what you think is good, you are a son or daughter of destruction. You are not only being destroyed in your life like the Antichrist, but you destroy others around you.

I was reading a story this week about a young girl who struggled with this idea of God's moral code. She grew up as a missionary kid in Kenya. When she was a teenager, probably because she had seen so much darkness, so much pain, so many innocent people dying and suffering, much more than most any of us here have seen, she started questioning God's love, God's care, God's goodness. By the time she was in her twenties and in college, she had rejected Christianity altogether. But after she got a little older, she began to understand.

One night she was in a philosophical discussion with a young man about the existence of God. He was arguing that morality was relative, different for every culture and every person. He wrapped up his argument concluding that morals are totally subjective, and therefore, God is unnecessary.

This young lady found herself arguing that if morals were totally subjective, then you can't say Hitler was wrong; you can't say it is unjust to let babies starve to death like she saw happen in Kenya; you can't say *anything* is wrong! She found she was forced into accepting an objective moral standard as well as the possibility that the source of this moral standard was divine. She realized that she was taking the first step back to real belief in God.

She later said that when people asked her what drove her out of the church and what drove her back, the answer to both questions is the same. She left the church in part because she was mad at God about human suffering and injustice. And she came back to church because of that same struggle. She began to realize that you couldn't even talk about justice without standing inside a theistic framework.

In a naturalistic framework, an orphan in the slums of Nairobi could only be explained in terms of survival of the fittest, that we are all just animals slumming in a godless world fighting for space and resources. The idea of justice doesn't really mean anything. To talk about justice, you have to talk about objective morality, and to talk about objective morality you have talk about God.

She was beginning to understand that, as much as you and I struggle with it and have a hard time understanding it, there is a moral code—written on your heart and written in the pages of Scripture. That's why we study the Scriptures—so we can follow God's moral code, and if we do, we will be blessed.

Did you notice here that this young woman, in her search for truth, was taking steps? Have you taken those steps, or are you stuck?

At this point in the story, after Jacob speaks to his boys, warning them and encouraging them, he dies. We turn to Genesis 50.

God's Purpose Is Good for You

> Then Joseph fell on his father's face and wept over him and kissed him. And Joseph commanded his servants the physicians to embalm his father. So the physicians embalmed Israel. Forty days were required for it, for that is how many are required for embalming. And the Egyptians wept for him seventy days. (Gen. 50:1–3)

> When Joseph's brothers saw that their father was dead, they said, "It may be that Joseph will hate us and pay us back for all the evil that we did to him." So they sent a message to Joseph, saying, "Your father gave this command before he died, 'Say to Joseph, Please forgive the transgression of your brothers and their sin, because they did evil to you.' And now, please forgive the transgression of the servants of the God of your father." Joseph wept when they spoke to him. His brothers also came and fell down before him and said, "Behold, we are your servants." But Joseph said to them, "Do not fear, for am I in the place of God? As for you, you meant evil against me, but God meant it for good, to bring it about that many people should be kept alive, as they are today. So do not fear; I will provide for you and your little ones." Thus he comforted them and spoke kindly to them. (50:15–21)

It is interesting that the brothers sent a messenger to Joseph. They were afraid to talk face-to-face to their little brother, Joseph. And they bring a message supposedly from their dead father, saying, "Forgive your brothers." Do you really think their dad actually said that? I think they made it up. I think Joseph saw through that charade, and that's why he wept when he heard the message.

Then his brothers come and fall down before him, presenting themselves as slaves. But Joseph tells them not to be afraid and asks them this question: "Am I in the place of God?" It reminds me of Romans 12:19—"Beloved, never avenge yourselves, but leave it to the wrath of God, for it is written, 'Vengeance is mine, I will repay, says the Lord.'"

Don't ever forget that verse. You can't live the Christian life otherwise. If you are out avenging yourself, getting even with those who have wronged you, you are *not* living the Christian life! And Joseph, way back in the Old Testament, long before Romans was ever written, says, "Am I God? I can't judge you. Vengeance is up to God."

I realize this is not an easy thing to do, whether it's the guy who cuts you off in traffic or the business associate who cheats you, your relative who betrays you or the Christian brother or sister who gossips about you. This is a difficult decision—but this might be the step you need to take right now to really walk with God.

And then we come to verse 20. Think about what this says: "As for you, you meant evil against me . . ." They came close to killing their little brother Joseph and instead sold him into slavery. His master's wife framed him and got him thrown into prison. The fellow prisoner he helped out agreed to speak up for him, but forgot. There are a lot of people who wronged him, but he keeps making this decision: "You meant it for evil against me, but"—the biggest "but" in the whole Bible!—"God meant it for good."

God meant it for good? Your brothers were going to kill you, and God meant it for good? You get sold into slavery, but God meant it for good? You get lied about and thrown in jail, but God meant it for good? It looks like Joseph is taking steps, too.

This is a huge philosophical dilemma—God uses *evil*? He uses evil for *good*? That may be hard to understand, but it's a basic theological concept you've got to grasp if you are going to be a Christian.

This was the secret that made Nelson Mandela great. When he became president of South Africa in 1994, instead of wreaking vengeance on all his enemies, he said, "Let's forgive each other." Really? After spending twenty-seven years in jail? That is outstanding. It is similar to Joseph's declaration: "You meant it for evil, but God meant it for good." This has got to be one of the strongest, most powerful statements in the entire Bible. And it's exactly what you need to hear right now, no matter what you are facing.

Alvin Plantinga, a professor of philosophy, was trying to explain the dilemma of how we can believe that God is good in the midst of evil and pain, and came up with an analogy from his camping experiences.

Imagine a little pup tent with flaps at each end. If you lift the flap and look in, you can safely say that there is no St. Bernard in the tent. Surely if there was one in there, we would see it. However, if you have ever gone camping up in Minnesota, you know that there are little bugs called "no-see-ums." They are so small you really can't see them, but you can feel their bite. So if you look in the pup tent and cannot see any "no-see-ums," that doesn't mean they aren't there.

Plantinga relates that to God and says it's a question of whether God's reasons for allowing evil are more like St. Bernards or more like "no-see-ums." God's reasons and thoughts are way above ours. Just because we don't know what they are doesn't mean they are not there. He concludes that with God's omniscience and our rather substantial intellectual limitations, it should not surprise us that God's reasons escape us.[2]

Often we think we have to figure it out. We struggle with difficulties in our lives or injustice in the world, and we get angry with God because we're really putting ourselves in the place of God, as if we would know what's good or bad. A lot of injustice that happens is not going to be straightened out until we get to glory.

In my years as a pastor, I have counseled hundreds of people. Some of their stories stand out in my mind, like that of one beautiful young woman and what she learned from a very difficult situation. When I first met her, you would have thought her life was perfect. She had a wonderful husband, they made a good living and they had a nice home and two wonderful children. They were Christians and were active in our church. But then, suddenly, her husband announced he was leaving. He had been having an affair with another woman.

Obviously, she and her children were devastated. But over the next several months, she started to take steps that would lead her out of this wasteland.

At first, she questioned God. Was this really His plan? How could it be? How could he just walk away? How could something good come from this? She was angry. She had no idea what was going to become of her and her children.

After several counseling sessions, she said that she was noticing changes—not in the situation, but in her heart. She still felt betrayed but she was beginning to let it all go to God. She told me she had started praying for her husband, praying that his heart would be healed, that he would come back to God, not just come back to her. She started planning for life without him and became more aware of God in her life. She was beginning to let it go—the anger, the bitterness, the hatred.

She felt drawn to the Word of God in a whole new way— as though it were the air she needed to live. She studied daily. It was starting to have an effect on her.

Things did not get significantly better over the next several months. Her husband was still with his girlfriend, her kids were still struggling with his absence, even acting out against her and the church and their faith. She had gone back to work, which meant the kids were now with sitters a lot and her time with them was limited. They had "lost" their dad and now she felt she was missing from their lives as well. She still loved this man, and she was still praying for him. And it still seemed unfair, but she was still seeking God.

Finances became a significant problem. Her house went up for sale to avoid foreclosure. She had no idea where they would move. Yet, in the middle of all this, she was starting to know God on a higher level. She could actually see His hand working in ways she had never imagined. You could see the change on her face. She was starting to find joy.

She shared with me that she had never really had to depend on God—not like this. And she was learning that He was trustworthy, that His words were true and that He could handle any situation she brought to Him. She realized that she was not alone and, in truth, she couldn't do this alone. But she could see that Jesus was holding her, comforting her, lifting her—even carrying her.

She came to the conclusion that she still wanted to see justice done, but not her justice—God's. She came to realize that her husband was God's problem and that she needed only to be faithful. God would handle the rest.

The last time I spoke with her, she was excited! She saw God moving in miraculous ways and she was excited to see how this was all going to end. She knew the way ahead of her was going to be hard. She knew there would be hills and valleys—deep, dark valleys. But she had learned that the sun shines in the valleys as well as on the hills and that God was going to bring her and her children through. She was excited about who she was becoming and couldn't wait to see who she would be on the other side of this storm.

As the apostle Paul says, we are in a race, and it's hard. You run, you get tired, you feel like quitting, but you keep taking those steps, one by one by one, until you gain the victory. You will be tired but you will be energized by the experience. On the other side of the storm, you will be stronger, have more understanding and more trust. And when the next storm begins to brew, when the first drop of rain begins to fall, you will look up!

If you are going to live the Christian life, you've got to take steps. You stop stepping, you stop growing. You become stunted and immature; you're not going where you need to go. Whether you are going through divorce or going through a promotion, whether things are going great or things are going horribly, the big question in life will always be the same: What's the next step?

And that's how we conclude this book: what's your next step? You need to figure that out and take that step. God's asking you to trust Him in the midst of some situation or circumstance where you feel like you're under attack. But Joseph's statement, "You meant it for evil, but God meant it for good" just screams at us. Will you believe God's moral code is good for you? Will you believe He is good? Will you come to the conviction that God has a purpose in all this? In the end, you will understand when you get to glory.

But right now the big question is, "What's my next step?" Is it painful, is it uphill, is it difficult? *Yes!* But take that step now. God promises you won't regret it. Joseph never did.

Prayer

Lord, what is my next step? Show me, Lord. Maybe You already have and I haven't taken it. Give me the courage and grace to put one foot in front of the other and step. I am willing, Lord. It may be hard, it may be uphill, but I am trusting in You. I've made the decision. I'm going to do it. Your morality is good. Your purpose is good. You are good. I trust Your goodness. In my heart and mind I know that I want You to make me like Joseph. I want to have such confidence in You that it's unshakable. Guide my steps, Lord. I am Yours. In the name of Jesus Christ I pray. Amen.

Notes

Chapter 1

1. Pete Scazzero, *The Emotionally Healthy Church* (Grand Rapids: Zondervan, 2003).
2. Elisabeth Elliot, *A Path Through Suffering* (Ventura: Regal Books, 1990).

Chapter 2

1. Haddon Robinson, *What Jesus Said About Successful Living* (Grand Rapids: Discovery House Publishers, 1991).

Chapter 3

1. John Piper, *The Godward Life* (Colorado Springs: Multnomah, 1997).

Chapter 4

1. Leona Choy, *Powerlines: What Great Evangelicals Believed About The Holy Spirit* (Camp Hill: Christian Publications, 1990).

Chapter 6

1. C.S. Lewis, *A Grief Observed* (New York: Harper & Row, 1961).
2. C.S. Lewis, *The Problem of Pain* (New York: HarperOne, 2001).

Chapter 8

1. John Piper, *A Godward Life* (Colorado Springs: Multnomah, 1997).

2. Timothy Keller, *Walking With God Through Pain and Suffering* (New York: Penguin Group, 2013).

Chapter 9

1. Max Lucado, *You'll Get Through This* (Nashville: Thomas Nelson, 2013).
2. Tim Hansel, "Great Lady," *Morrison County Record.* May 20, 2000. Online at http://archives.ecmpublishers. info/2000/05/20/great-lady/

Chapter 10

1. Gene Getz, *Life Essential Study Bible* (Nashville, TN: Holman Bible Publishers, 2011).

Chapter 11

1. C.S. Lewis, *Mere Christianity* (New York, NY: HarperOne, 1980).
2. Alvin Plantinga, quoted in Timothy Keller, *Walking With God Through Pain and Suffering* (New York: Penguin Group, 2013).

PUBLICATIONS

Fort Washington, PA 19034

This book is published by CLC Publications, an outreach of CLC Ministries International. The purpose of CLC is to make evangelical Christian literature available to all nations so that people may come to faith and maturity in the Lord Jesus Christ. We hope this book has been life changing and has enriched your walk with God through the work of the Holy Spirit. If you would like to know more about CLC, we invite you to visit our website:

www.clcusa.org

To know more about the remarkable story of the founding of CLC International we encourage you to read

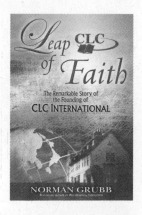

LEAP OF FAITH

Norman Grubb

Paperback
Size 5¹/₄ x 8, Pages 248
ISBN: 978-0-87508-650-7
ISBN (*e-book*): 978-1-61958-055-8